Praise for

JOURNEY

"I have known Libby since she was born... as we are sisters! And that makes me qualified, more than most, to be able to recommend her to you! Libby is one of the most pure-hearted, passionate followers of Jesus that I know. Hers is a life of worship. In her moments of greatest joy and success, she worships. In the deepest depths, you will find her worshipping. I have had the privilege of knowing Libby personally, but you can have the same privilege by meeting her (and her heart for worship) in this book..."

- Jilly Schein
YWAM, Capetown, SA

"Libby has been a very dear friend of mine for the past seven years, and our two families have been very close, doing life together for much of this time. This has given me a very real picture of the way Libby lives her life, and I can testify to her integrity of heart and her very real relationship with Jesus, which spills out into a beautiful ministry of love towards others.

Both Libby and Wayne have contributed and are still contributing hugely into the New Zealand worship world, as well as in Europe, USA, Asia and Australia, working with church teams, to encourage and lift individuals to reach their full potential in God, in the whole realm of worship. Libby and Wayne are leaders who lead by serving. This is the premise by which they lead others, and I believe is the key to their authority to teach others.

Libby, though operating at a high level within the church life has the ability to also care for the one. Her ministry is a ministry of love, and she gives of herself openly to those who need mentoring and care within her sphere.

Above all, Libby is Mum to Gracie and Josh - she has overseen their lives beautifully, prayed for them, lavished love on them, and they have grown to be young people who love God and the church, and are strongly pursuing Jesus' call on their own lives.

I have had the pleasure of walking through some of the journeys Libby speaks of in her book and have watched her hold on to God, never wavering in her faith even when life has been challenging. Libby walks what she talks, her life is an expression of worship and sacrifice, and she loves her Jesus."

- Karoline Marshall
Auckland, New Zealand

"Libby Huirua's authenticity and love for Jesus truly resonates in and through her life. She has served in our local church for many years and has impacted New Zealand and the nations around the globe through worship. Her ministry has definitely stood the test of time, her passion to bring God's presence into every area of our lives is a message that is a clear mark on Libby's life. This book will bring you closer to the Father's heart towards you and will impact you on a deeper level."

- Pastor Kathy Monk
Senior Minister, Equippers Church
Auckland, New Zealand

"Journey is a book filled with gold that has come from the life of a true seeker and worshipper of Jesus. It is an invitation to explore the heart of God through the experiences and songs that have arisen from a listening and attentive heart. I have known Libby Huirua for many years and have been privileged to see her passion for worship and leading others into God's presence in a very up-close and personal way. This book is a true reflection of her authentic, raw and personal faith.

I have the greatest respect and admiration for Libby - not only for the way she has developed her gifts and calling as a worship leader and songwriter, but also as a wife, a mother, a friend and leader. Her message and her songs have risen from her personal

journey with God and she openly invites us into this adventure. There is so much wisdom, practical advice and encouragement on every page and I am confident this book will draw you into a deeper and more meaningful walk with God, imparting wisdom, insight and much joy as you read it.
Let the Journey begin…"

                - Pastor Helen Burns
                  Relate Church, Vancouver, BC
                  Author, Television Host
                  International Speaker

JOURNEY

LIBBY HUIRUA

Libby Huirua

Copyright 2014 Libby Huirua
All rights reserved.
ISBN: 1502835797
ISBN-13: 978-1502835796

JOURNEY

DEDICATION

To my Jesus - my greatest love, my highest joy. I can never repay You, so I simply say, 'I am Yours!'

JOURNEY

CONTENTS

Acknowledgements   11

1. The Journey Begins   17
2. A Season to Grow   27
3. Deeper   39
4. God Knows What He's Doing   55
5. How Can I Not Sing?   63
6. It All Begins in the Mind   71
7. Expensive Worship   95
8. Created for One-ness   109
9. My Soul Sings   121
10. Living Building Stones   135
11. It's All About Jesus   147
12. Agents of Change   165

ACKNOWLEDGEMENTS

There are so many people I would want to acknowledge at the beginning of this book. People who have walked my life road with me, who have spoken into my life, who have just been incredible friends and mentors… but the list of acknowledgments would possibly end up longer than the book. So, I will just say I am so very thankful for so many life relationships that are deep, sweet and strong… and you know who you are!

However, there is need to specifically acknowledge a few…

Waynie - you have been my best friend from about the first week we met, in 1986. You became my soul mate, well before you became my life mate, and it was your vulnerability and soft heart towards God that was the greatest attraction for me. That has never changed. I am so grateful that God had plans for us, and the adventure our life has been together, has been so very cool! We've been through some pretty hard stuff for sure, but I couldn't have wished for anyone, or any life, better. Your love, kindness, consistency, and heart for me and others, far outweighs the socks left lying on the lounge floor! Thank you for always believing in me, always challenging me, always loving me and most importantly, always loving our God. The future is bright! I love you…

Gracie - my world was turned upside down, and inside out when God gave us you! I was changed forever. I have always known you were not ours to own, but leant to us for this life on earth, and it has been the utmost privilege to be your Mama. You are beautiful inside and out, you are strong, you are a leader, a beautiful worshipper, you are confident, you are so very kind, and you know and love Jesus. I couldn't have prayed for anyone better in a daughter. I love you…

Josh - where do I start? You are a young man of passion, justice, intelligence and sensitivity. You know your Jesus and you want to serve and honour Him. For that, I couldn't be more thankful! You make me laugh like no one else does, you are quirky and just a little bit coolly odd! I love that you know who you are and you are definitely a world changer. I love you buddy and I'm so proud to be your Mum!

To my Mama, and Dad. Thank you for providing the best possible foundation for me to launch off. Your stability, love and commitment to our family was strong and truly made all of us who we are. I am so very grateful for the sacrifices you both made to give us what we needed to thrive and flourish, but not so much that we didn't know how to grow up well! I love you and am forever grateful to you both...

Jilly, my best friend and sis. You make me laugh, and you are one of the consistent joys in my life. I know you don't remember singing Jesus songs around the house, but I saw Jesus in you, I wanted to follow Him because of you, and have seen Him in you ever since! Thank you for being the best sister and friend a girl could ever have, or wish for. You are truly one of my greatest heroes... and I love you!

Pastors Bruce and Helen Monk and Sam and Kathy Monk - what a family! You have believed in us, spoken into us, encouraged and championed us. You have shepherded and stewarded an incredible church, and ministries have been birthed from Equippers that we are so very honoured to be a part of. Thank you for all you have spoken into our lives. It is an absolute honour to call you pastors and friends, and we love serving under you!

Finally, the majority of this book (and Wayne's!) was written over the summer of 2012/2013 and there were a number of people who helped make that possible for us. People who love and believe in us, and who chose to partner with us to bring this to reality. 'Thank you' sounds so lightweight on paper, but in the heart, they are two weighty and life changing words. We couldn't have done this without you all, truly. Thank you… may you be blessed accordingly in every area of your lives!

Soane and Michelle Tonga
Dan Protheroe
Stu and Margot Shutt
Willie and Desi Levy and Masterton Equippers Church
Dawn Bauer
Wayne and Raewyn Mortensen
Carl and Kirsty Green and Tauranga Equippers Church
Greg and Amy Lynas
Andy Pearce
Brent and Alex Smart
Leon and Ruthie Cooke
Reg and Andy Khoo
David and Karen Ruddock
Sandi Gasperini
Dan and Jen Gray and Gisborne Equippers Church
Cherith and Eddie Vahakolo
Don and Jill Smith and Pukekohe Community Church
Susanna and Andrew Wilson
Fitz and Aig Su'a-Huirua
Neli and Tina Atiga
Paul and Alicia Zaia
Pete and Annie Lamb
Elaine Reber
Lyle and Debi Penisula and Hawkes Bay Equippers Church

And some final notes of gratitude: To the incredible Hannah Marchant and Helene Jordi, for your 'arty' touch!
To Vince Mills, for hours of painful and selfless editing…
To Sarah Sims, for lending me your scholarly wisdom and insight…
And to Rebi Wellauer, for your referencing genius…

I appreciate you all greatly!

Journey...

"And how blessed all those in whom You live, whose lives become roads You travel; they wind through lonesome valleys, come upon brooks, discover cool springs brimming with rain! God-travelled, these roads curve up the mountain, and at the last turn - Zion! God in full view!" (Psalm 84:5-7 MSG)

Life is simply an invitation. An invitation to a journey. With a travel companion you have not yet met. The travel companion is the driver, and you are the hitch-hiker. As the hitch-hiker, you are possibly aware of your final destination, but have no real idea of the route you will take to get there. In the end, it's not really about the destination, but more about the journey. Sometimes a rutted country lane, sometimes a much travelled freeway, but there's always a road stretching before you and an invitation to travel it...

Chapter One
The Journey Begins...

The book you hold in your hands is a small synopsis of my life. It's an expression of what I feel has made me who I am, and I have written it down, really out of the recognition that we, who are older, have a responsibility to share our journey - mistakes and triumphs - with the generations to follow! But in the telling there's a desire and longing that you would see past the 'me' and into the 'He' who made me.

As I started on the journey of writing this book, I asked my daughter, Gracie, whether anyone would actually want to read it. I have read so many powerful testimonies over the years of people being rescued out of horrific and heartbreaking situations in their lives - physical and mental abuse, drug and alcohol addiction, gripping fear, recurrent miscarriages, and tragic loss of loved ones' lives, financial ruin, and debilitating mental disorders. These things have not really been part of my journey before or since accepting the invitation to the journey... I have, by the grace of God, been saved FROM those things.

But I have also read incredible stories of miraculous healing, instant freedom from all sorts of bondage, restoration of relationships, and lives radically turned around. Again, I have no dramatic testimony of these sorts. Yes, of course life has been real - I have experienced pain as everyone does, and there have been some experiences and challenges that, in time, I know will be written into another story. But THIS story is simply the journey into the heart of my Creator, and discovering and developing a relationship of freedom, and intimacy with His heart, not with the 'rules'. And, therefore, it is a story no less real or powerful...

People have often told me that I live a blessed life, and it's true, I do. God has been very gracious and good to me.

But nothing worthwhile is ever forged without the press of trial and challenge, and my journey has had many of those life lessons written into its very fabric. So, what follows in this book, are God experiences on my life road, journeying to the heart of my Father, interlaced with songs that have been written on that journey. These stories and songs are not necessarily in chronological order. Some of the songs were written in the midst of the story being told, some were not, yet they relate, and some not even written by myself, yet they have been special to me and therefore, capture the essence of the journey.

But first, let's start at the beginning…

Take a breath…

"I was lost but You found me in a heartbeat
Turned me round with the sound of my whispered name
I am Yours, forever changed
Lord, You saw me and saved me in my greatest need
You saw me, unformed, and Your whisper came:
'you are Mine, forever Mine'
    God of my rescue, my hope's found in Christ alone
    God of my rescue, my life's found in Christ, my home
Breathe life into me,
Breathe life into me,
Breathe life until I'm overflowing.
Overwhelm me…"

- 'Breathe',[1]

I was born on January 6, 1967, and grew up in Eastbourne, Wellington, New Zealand. A beachside paradise 'down-under'. I was the youngest of five children - the 'baby of the family' as my parents still introduced me to people, well into my adult years. My older siblings would say I was spoilt, but I beg to differ. As the youngest, I had the privilege (at the age of about three I remember), of playing the role of 'pet tiger' in a game with my three older sisters and brother. This involved laying under a bed for the whole game and not making a sound. Spoilt? I don't think so! My father called me his 'little autumn leaf', (I think that was a nice name for *"Whoops… we didn't see you coming!"*)

My mother and father met on a ship, sailing passage between England and New Zealand. A fourth generation New Zealander, and daughter of a general surgeon, my mother was heading overseas to see Europe with her cousin, after completing her training as a physiotherapist. My father was an officer in the British Merchant Navy, stationed on that ship. Mum and her cousin were seated at Dad's table every night for dinner, and I guess there's something about a man in dress uniform because, somewhere during that six-week journey, they fell in love, and the rest is history. Dad left the British Merchant Navy, and emigrated to New Zealand, while Mum stayed in England to travel and complete her term as a physiotherapist. They saw each other for an entire six weeks of their two-year engagement and then, once Mum returned to New Zealand, they were married in Ashburton where she had grown up. Not long after their wedding, they moved to Wellington and lived in a little seaside cottage, where my eldest brother was born two years later.

I had a pretty idyllic childhood - Mum and Dad had a stable and committed marriage, our needs were taken care of, and we had strong family values and morals instilled in us. We all went to the local primary school, and the beach was our ever-changing and endless playground. We grew up in a time when you played outside until dark, climbed trees (and, of course, inevitably broke a bone or two in the process), rode bikes, took 'risks' on the rocks by the sea as the tide came in and, as long as you were home in time for dinner, all was well. We could buy four lollies for one cent, and a whole packet of fish and chips for just 15 cents! I remember having a black and white television when I was quite young and there was only one viewing channel. On Sunday evenings we were allowed to watch Disneyland but that was it. There were no shops open on Sunday either for that matter -

Sunday truly was considered a special and important day of the week.

My maternal Grandma passed away when I was only six months old, and I think, because of that, I held a special place in my Grandpa's heart. He moved to Eastbourne and lived near our school and, on the odd occasion when I was sick and Mum was at work, I would go to his flat and he would take me out driving around the Eastbourne Bays road and buy me ice-cream. He was a kind and gentle man, he would write me letters whenever he went away for a holiday, and I was always fascinated by his big surgeon's hands. He was one of my favourite people in the whole world, and his passing away, when I was eight years old, affected me greatly. My English gran emigrated to New Zealand after my grandfather passed away. She lived just down the road from us, and would come for Sunday roast lunch every week. She was almost completely blind, so we would take turns walking her home, and would recite funny little English poems together. I was privileged to grow up with a very strong sense of the honouring of generations, and the blessing that was.

Our house was situated on a little circular hill terrace, and backed onto six different properties. We had elderly neighbours who put a ladder against their fence so that I could climb over and visit them, without having to run around the road to their front door. Mrs Hayley was an artist and a poet, and even wrote and published a poem about Libby, *'the little girl with eyes so blue'*, who would come and brighten up their day with songs and laughter. It was they who introduced me to drinking tea at the age of three, and I learnt of the undeniable pleasures of caffeine at the age of ten! One of my very enjoyable memories as a child would be hearing the call *"Anyone for coffee?"* ring out throughout our house at precisely 10.30 on a Saturday morning, and we'd all stop what we were doing and gather in the kitchen for coffee and something yummy Mum had baked. We attended a Presbyterian Church and went to Sunday school (my brother was apparently adept at climbing out of the window and escaping to home). Mum was the initiator of church attendance, while Dad would sometimes attend the Christmas morning service, but I wouldn't necessarily say we had an overtly Christian upbringing. We didn't say bedtime prayers or 'grace' before meals, so I would say I knew about God, but that was about it.

Perception shapes everything...

It is easy, upon reflection, to look at your childhood through rose-coloured spectacles. So let me give you a little perspective. I firmly believe that our perception of life and our situations will shape and mould our responses to that life. Although I was physically loved and well cared for, I do remember a deep sense of loneliness growing up. It was NOTHING to do with anyone's treatment of me, or lack of care on anyone else's part, but completely to do with my personality wiring, probably my place/order in our family, and my perception of my young life. I just had a gnawing, pretty constant feeling that I, somehow, didn't 'fit' my life. There was quite an age difference between me and my next oldest sister (remember I was the unexpected 'autumn leaf' my parents hadn't planned!), and my brother had left home by the time I was six years old. Because of the age difference between us all, I was often left to play by myself and, for someone who loved the buzz of people around her, this made me feel very lonely. Understandably added to that, in order to help provide for a large family, Mum also returned to work while I was still in preschool, so I was often looked after by others after kindergarten, reinforcing the feeling that I was a bit of a nuisance even though that was completely untrue. I remember often feeling scared and alone - I didn't like dark rooms, I didn't like rainy days, I hated my first week of school, and I was often fearful of getting into trouble or making mistakes. Consequently, I hid what I was feeling a lot of the time, and felt I needed to strive to be 'good'.

The velcro spirit...

I would also pick up atmospheres all around me - changes in the weather, and even in the physical properties of light and dark, would affect me. I remember, as a six-year old, sitting at the bottom of our staircase while a very stiff Wellington wind blew outside. I'm sure there were other people at home, but I do remember feeling completely alone, and hating the sound of the wind, and the darkness of our hallway in the late afternoon fading light. Just those external, physical properties affected my emotions.

I could sense the feeling in a room, and the emotion behind people's conversations, and my feelings would reflect the atmosphere around me. Still now, I have dreams, where everything looks completely normal, but then one physical property will change - the light will alter, or a road will start sloping - and I know I'm about to enter a nightmare. I have learnt how to wake myself up out of those ones...

Now, if you asked my siblings, they would have had their different impressions of growing up in our family, but I just often felt fearful and out of place. I remember having a friend in primary school who was extremely strong and possessive over me, refusing to let me speak to other girls in my class, or go to their houses to play. I knew there was something very wrong about this girl's controlling demands on my friendship, and it really scared me, making me feel sick, trapped and isolated, but I also felt I couldn't really talk to anyone about it, or ask for help. Along with that, there were also a couple of incidents in those earlier formative years, when some older men treated me inappropriately - not abuse as such, but suggestive comments and visual attention towards me at a vulnerable age, which again, left me feeling fearful, alone and unable to talk about it openly with anyone.

I just felt things so very deeply, and there were often emotions within me that I didn't like or understand but were part of this perceptive and sensitive nature. I remember one particularly poignant incident, years later when I was in high school. A new boy showed up in my maths class at the beginning of the year, having transferred from another school, and I had a bit of a teenage crush on him - he was a really nice guy, very intelligent, quiet, and a bit shy, but genuine and kind. Possibly he felt a deep need to be accepted in this new school, because I noticed him getting into the wrong crowd, drinking and partying and, over the course of a few months, he had changed dramatically. He started going backwards in his schooling, his behaviour changed markedly, and he had become really hard as a person. One night, a friend and I felt a real urgency to pray for him, and I remember earnestly interceding, *"God would you show yourself to him tonight? Wherever he is, do whatever it takes to bring him to a knowledge and understanding of You."* It doesn't take much imagination to understand how horrified I was, when I got a call the next morning saying he had been killed in a car accident that very night. For a long time, even though knowing God is gracious and was in control of his destiny, I still carried the heaviness and guilt of wondering whether I had somehow, unconsciously caused his death by my prayer.

I felt so uneasy with this perceptive ability to sense atmospheres and read situations. In hindsight, with adult maturity, I recognise this as being one of the hallmarks of having a prophetic and discerning nature but, as a young one growing up, I didn't understand it at all. I just somehow felt out of place, and often unhappy and fearful, with emotions that I didn't understand. It was as if the atmosphere would just stick to me… like velcro.

So, I knew in my head I was loved, and had people around me, but my heart told me I was more of a nuisance and alone. Again, I feel the need to reiterate that this wasn't anyone's fault, but my perception alone. I needed to really feel I belonged and was loved, not just in my head, but in the very deepest part of my soul…

Invitation…

When my sister Jilly, was 13, she got involved in an organisation called Youth for Christ, but it was when she was 16 that I remember sensing for the first time, that something about her seemed to have changed. I couldn't put my finger on it, but I knew that she had discovered something that I really wanted and needed. You have to understand, I was always trying to be a good kid, and grew up with a very keen awareness of right and wrong. In fact, I stole a grape once from outside our local greengrocer's, and felt desperately guilty about it, so sensitive was my conscience. But even from a young age, I sensed a gaping void, a divide between who I was, and who and what I felt I should be. So when Jilly told me she had become a Christian, I could tell that she had changed, and I knew I needed what she had. There was an instinctive awareness that she had found truth and freedom. I didn't know why, but her new disposition made me angry and irritable. She would sing Christian songs around our house, and the lyrics made me feel even more out of place and angry. I felt as if she was 'getting at me' on purpose - the only way I can describe it, is it felt like something in the very deepest part of me, was at war with her, and I hated that feeling. One afternoon, after we had been visiting Gran, that horrible tension I felt towards Jilly in my heart reached boiling point. We had a fight, I exploded in anger at her (I think I punched her in the arm, I was feeling so pent-up mad!), and stormed off home. In the natural I was just an angry kid who'd had an argument with her sister, but in the spirit, I was poised on the edge of eternity, about to make the most important decision of my life. I was tired of feeling displaced, so I gave up the struggle and, that hot summer afternoon, in January 1979, while I was doing my paper run, I simply asked Jesus into my heart. I don't know how I knew that asking Jesus into my heart was something I should do. There was no minister preaching a sermon in a church service, no worship team leading any song, and no one to lead me through the 'sinner's prayer'. I was just a 12-

year old girl, delivering her papers, and the Creator of the Universe stopped me in my tracks and extended an invitation to me… and I simply, and fully accepted it.

> "I was lost, but You found me in a heartbeat
> Turned me round, with the sound of my whispered name,
> I am Yours, forever changed.
> Lord, You saw me and saved me in my greatest need.
> You saw me, unformed, and Your whisper came:
> 'you are Mine, forever Mine.'"

I heard the beckoning whisper of my Father that day, *"You are Mine!"* And, as I asked Jesus into my heart and to take charge of my life, I physically felt Him rush in. Joy and peace flooded my soul. It was singularly the happiest moment of my young life to that point. The anger, and that feeling of warring in my spirit, was gone. I remember racing home that afternoon, hardly being able to contain the joy and freedom I felt in my heart. Oh, the miracle of a heart born again, is impossible to rationalise or explain to someone else - nothing had changed on the outside, yet everything was different inside. I was a changed person. I was ALIVE. I was FREE. I was NEW!

> "But for you who welcome Him, in whom He dwells - even though you still experience all the limitations of sin - you yourself experience life on God's terms. It stands to reason, doesn't it, that if the alive-and-present God who raised Jesus from the dead moves into your life, He'll do the same thing in you that He did in Jesus, bringing you alive to Himself? When God lives and breathes in you (and He does, as surely as He did in Jesus), you are delivered from that dead life. With His Spirit living in you, your body will be as alive as Christ's!" (Romans 8:10-11 MSG)[2]

This was my reality that day and I can still remember that feeling as clearly as if it were yesterday. It still brings tears to my eyes, when I think of the goodness and kindness of Almighty God, stopping to encounter me, just a 12-year old girl, simply because He wanted me to be His. And I KNEW I belonged to Him… I had accepted His invitation, and the journey had begun!

Balanced scales…

God doesn't play favourites. He doesn't regard, or rescue one individual compared to another based on their apparent need of Him. The fact is, we ALL NEED GOD. We're all created with a longing to be one with our Creator, whether we're aware of it or not, and there's a point in each of our lives when we wake up to that truth. You see I used to think life began at conception and, once physically born nine months later, a child really began to live. I know, now, that I had been conceived in the heart of the Father, long before I ever came into existence, and although my life physically began at conception, and I was physically born nine months later, I only truly began to live at 12 years of age, when I 'woke up' to God's full intent for me - a relationship of one-ness and intimacy with my Creator. I am so thankful that He extended to me the invitation to take the journey of a lifetime… of eternity… and I jumped on board. I would not exchange this journey for anything.

My biggest joy would be that, as you read this book and listen to the songs, you'd encounter a deeper understanding of the intimacy and freedom YOU were created for.

Chapter Two
A Season To Grow...

It always amuses me that even though we profess to be saved by faith, acknowledging that we are absolutely nothing without Him, we still spend a lot of our life unconsciously living by another set of measures. We declare that we can't do anything to earn our salvation or His love, yet we strive to be good, unconsciously thinking we need to chalk up 'brownie points' in heaven, comparing and measuring our progress by others' successes or failures. And tragically, more than anything, we desperately try to gain worth, acceptance and identity from so many other things, than just His unconditional love for us. I know this sanctification business is a lifelong journey, but we'd save ourselves a whole lot of time and energy if we'd just give up the fight, dare to take God at His Word, and live what He says!

After I became a Christian at the age of 12, I definitely felt His presence with me keenly. I had a hunger to know more of God, and to be known by Him. This was something that just seemed so natural to me - I had been awakened to the real meaning of life and my purpose within it all. I would often take my Bible to high school with me, and read it before classes started for the day, as I had somehow learnt straight away that there was huge power in the words written on those pages, and they could actually be applied to my everyday life.

Youth revival in our nation...

Youth for Christ was really booming as an organisation in the late 1970's and into the 1980's, catering to a need that a lot of church youth groups just weren't meeting. It was exciting, relevant, and fun, and met that need for belonging which every young person, especially in their teenage years, yearns for. So I got really involved in YFC in Wellington - Campus Life Clubs, Insight groups (small Bible study groups), camps, and monthly rallies in the Wellington Town Hall. I wasn't aware of it at the time, but Youth for Christ was part of a huge revival amongst teenagers in New Zealand in the 80's and 90's, and I was very much caught up in that move of God. I will be forever grateful to the leaders within YFC, and also for some very dear people in our Presbyterian Church, who taught, mentored and discipled me in the ways of living the Christian life. That very strong foundation of meetings, clubs, camps and rallies - simply connection - contributed hugely towards keeping me grounded all the way through my high school years. But, I also somehow learnt that more than anything, beyond all these meetings, clubs, camps and rallies, the most important thing was a personal, daily, devotional life with God - 'one-on-one' alone time with my Father. And that was my life-line.

So I formed that habit from a young age - reading the Bible, praying, and memorising Bible verses that applied to my everyday situations. And it was through my growing personal relationship with Jesus that I started to realise, with absolute wonder, that God just wanted to spend time with me because He loved me. And He actually wanted me to hang out with Him because He wanted to be loved BY me in return. In uncluttered, basic teenage understanding... God just adored me, as I was right then, not as I thought I needed to be!

Contradiction...

However, I mentioned in the introductory chapter of this book, that I lived with that gnawing sense of loneliness, and feeling like a misfit as a younger child. That was nobody's fault, it was just the way I perceived life. That deep sensitivity was both a positive thing, with my heightened awareness of God and His presence, and a very negative thing, as I was affected by atmospheres and people's responses all around me. This sensitivity and feeling out of place, plus a few words spoken to me at a formative age about the way I looked, shaped the way I thought and felt about myself. These thoughts and feelings began to define who I was, to the point that, into my teenage years, I really battled with low self-esteem and feeling like I needed to measure up to the girls who I believed were beautiful, with perfect figures. A senseless and time-wasting pursuit, believe me.

So, I had become a Christian and on the one hand, I absolutely knew God loved me. But, at another much deeper level, I found it hard to love myself, or accept that others could love me. This contradiction between the absolute truth of God's love for me, and the lack of my own love for myself, caused constant internal conflict. To others, I came across as bubbly, outgoing, fun, caring and genuine. And, in a sense, I was all of those things. But inside, I was insecure, self-conscious, distrusting, envious and fearful. And I was ALL of those things too. The public persona that people saw, and the Libby that I never really let others see, battled with each other constantly. I guess this is true of all of us really, isn't it? Especially in our younger, less mature state. We unconsciously project an image of ourselves - the parts of ourselves that we assume people will like and accept, and we hide away the rest that isn't quite so acceptable or loveable. But God saw all of it! The very difficult thing was, I couldn't see the connection between God's love for me, and the absolute need to love and accept myself. I had no trouble believing that God loved me, because in my mind, His love was independent of me. He was God, and it was His nature to love, whether I thought I was loveable or not, so I never doubted it. And I took great comfort in that - it was a relief. Yet I couldn't love myself - in fact I unconsciously clung to that insecurity like a contradictory security blanket. And I would constantly swing between two camps - feeling deliciously accepted and safe in my relationship with God, but feeling vulnerable and out of place when I was just me. Two opinions cannot cohabit comfortably, so clearly something needed to change.

Until we find our true worth and identity in God's love alone, we will find it in a substitute, or sometimes many different substitutes. God's intent and heart has always been to bring us to that place where He alone is our source and our delight, and He will gently but definitely challenge those areas, relationships, and things which are subtly taking His rightful place in our hearts. It's not because He is egotistical and self-centred, in fact He's anything but! But He is very aware of how quickly self-absorbed and inward we become when we are finding our primary satisfaction and joy in something other than a relationship with Him. Well, in the midst of feeling so low in myself, I realised that singing was something I could do and was good at, and I unconsciously started using it as a measuring rod for my worth.

An idol?

Music was always a part of our home - there was always some sort of music being played on a record player or radio in the house. I always remember Dad whistling or humming a tune, and he would take us to musicals put on by the Wellington Operatic Society whenever he could. Even at the age of three, my sister and I would set up chairs on our back lawn, invite our neighbours over, and perform concerts for them with a five-stringed guitar (we didn't realise we could put a sixth string on!) So even though I went through the, *'I'm going to be a hairdresser or a vet'* phase (my poor cat was mercilessly tied to a trolley for make-believe surgical procedures), deep down, all I wanted to do was be a singer. I was often late for school in my later primary years because, once everyone had left the house for work and high school, I would put a record on in the lounge, turn up the volume, grab my soap-on-a-rope microphone (or hairbrush), and get lost in my dream of touring the world as some famous guys' background vocal singer.

When I became a Christian, naturally I decided I was going to sing for Jesus. I was going to be like Amy Grant and tour the world. At 14 years of age, I was asked to sing a solo for the first time in a Youth for Christ rally in the Wellington Town Hall. For an insecure and self-conscious 14 year-old, this was a huge deal. There were probably around 1500 people there and, though I was terrified, something in me was ALIVE as I sang. This led to me throwing myself into every opportunity to be involved in music and singing - I helped lead 'song times' in the rallies (which were crowd participation fun choruses), and was fully involved throughout high school with musicals and performance music classes, choirs and smaller singing groups, which I loved. There was also the opportunity to be in a couple of bands with YFC, performing at summer beach outreaches - again, I fully believed my main focus was Jesus and singing FOR Him. I also clearly remember at the age of about 18, helping to lead some worship at a reasonably small and intimate Christian camp, and being so overcome in God's presence, sobbing on my knees, that I had to be gently 'encouraged' off the stage! It was one of my earliest real encounters in worship and, though I didn't fully understand it, it felt like 'home' to me…

However, as I said, unbeknownst to me, co-existing alongside this desire to serve and love God, and use my gifting to honour Him, was this hidden need and drive to get worth from the very thing I wanted to serve Him with. It was a very real need to be appreciated and receive accolade for myself. And this was completely driven by my low self-esteem and poor self-image. If I couldn't be thin and beautiful like my friends, then at least I could sing and get some worth from that. It's only the journey and hindsight that revealed this hidden agenda to me because, at the time, I didn't even vaguely recognise it for what it was. I am so thankful for the kindness, patience and graciousness of God to allow me to walk the journey with Him. I guess this is largely why I am so passionate about communicating with singers who yearn to be known as 'singers', rather than simply recognising their gift as a vehicle to bring people closer to Jesus - especially in the worship arena.

Turn in the road...

Deep down, I knew I wasn't wired for university and a career in the secular arena, yet after finishing high school, I decided that university was the logical step in my 'growing up'. So, off I went to Victoria University, and started studying Commerce and Business Administration, thinking the degree would secure me a job - talk about 'square-peg-in-a-round-hole'! After that first year my parents could see I wasn't happy, and gave me the complete freedom to follow my dream. I'm so thankful for parents who gently guided, but never forced or controlled my decisions. I auditioned and got accepted for Y-One, a Youth for Christ touring team that trained for four months, and then toured the many high schools of New Zealand for six months. I had no idea when I auditioned, what God had in store for that year. It was to be a hallmark year that would forever be a milestone in my life both spiritually and physically.

Wayne, after spending one year at Massey University in Palmerston North, studying Physics (again, square peg, round hole!), was also accepted for this team. This was where we met, and we became best friends, though with a strict 'no-relationships-in-ministry' policy in place, we didn't start dating until 18 months later. This year on Y-One was an incredible year for me where my personal relationship with God grew in leaps and bounds. Along with ministry training, we had daily devotions as a team, and Jeff Todd, the Director of the whole ministry, taught me so much about devotion to God, and building a life where the foundation was completely Jesus and nothing else. Wayne and I both honour him to this day, as being one of our great mentors. Interestingly, too, Jeff sensed God tell him early on in that year, that Wayne and I would be together, married and working in ministry but, wisely, he never mentioned that to us until he officiated our wedding service, four years later!

God speaks...

I was water baptised at a Christian camp, when I was 18, and this was the first time I received a prophetic word through someone else, over my life. I had learnt how to hear God talk through the Bible in my quiet times, through sermons, and to recognise His personal voice to me from an early age, but it was during this year on Y-One that I heard God prophetically speak to me personally, for the first time, about my future. One morning after team devotions, I went away to spend some time with Him and, as I was praying, I heard Him speak. For me there's always a quickening of my heart when I sense God's voice, and a confirmation or knowing rises up in me, and even though it's within me, it's totally outside of me too - because I know it's Him speaking. Well this was the very first time I had felt that feeling, so I took note of it, and wrote down what I heard God speak:

"You are my chosen child. I want to do great things through you, but only when you are ready. You have to learn to keep your eyes on Me completely. Stop looking to the left and right, but keep your eyes firmly focused on Me. Don't strive to bring about what YOU want to happen in your future, just wait and let Me do the work in your life, and then it will be special, because My timing is perfect."

Springing right up alongside my ability to recognise God's voice, was my natural doubt, and I immediately started to think that maybe I had just made this up. I hated the thought that someone might think I was arrogant hearing this from God, and thinking I was 'the chosen one', so I didn't want to tell anyone about it. But I had been taught enough to know that I should test prophecy, so I asked God for confirmation. I felt Him say, *"Turn 15 pages in your daily reading book, and read what it says."*

I was reading a little devotional book called 'Our Daily Bread' at the time, so I flicked 15 pages in, and this is what I read:

"Looking back I see that God had a special work for me to do, and that His delayed answers were part of His preparation for a ministry of singing and writing... God's timing is always worth waiting for!"

I almost fell off my chair - God's answer was so specific, confirming again the desire of my heart to sing for Him. Even the mention of waiting for His timing, as God had told me specifically that His timing was perfect! In my excitement I kind of skipped over the part that told me not to strive to bring about what I wanted for the future, and I didn't think about the process needed to prepare me for it - I was just so excited to have heard Him speak and confirm that word so specifically.

Psalms 37:4 says:

"Delight yourself also in the Lord, and He shall give you the desires of YOUR heart." (NKJV)[1]

What a huge difference emphasis makes because now, in hindsight, I read that verse:

"... and HE shall give you the desires of your heart."

In other words, when we delight ourselves in Him, He will put the things that He desires in our heart, and HIS desires will become ours. And how graciously He prepares us in advance for that transition. I had spent a year developing my love for God, growing in my understanding of Him, wanting more of Him. And, by natural recourse, He decided when it was time to address this singing and insecurity issue, and realign my desires in the right way.

Profoundly altered...

So, it was at the end of that year, just when I knew God was calling me into full-time ministry, involving music and singing, that He put to death my dream to sing. Just like that. One day, singing for Jesus was all I wanted to do, the next day the desire to sing was completely gone from my heart. And I didn't like that feeling...

I can't put into words what happened, but there was a huge void in my heart - everything that I had been working towards - MY dreams, MY plans, my security and my worth - had been wrapped up in singing, and all of a sudden it was gone. There was no desire and no pleasure, just a gaping, aimless, visionless, purposeless, 'now what?' hole in my life... but I also felt somehow strangely relieved and free. Because during the course of that year, my love for God and my passion for His purposes and His heart, had become so much more important to me. How kind, and slightly tricky, God is to cause us to fall in love with Him before He starts gently addressing our stuff.

And I made a decision, that if God is God, and His Word says He has a plan and purpose for my life, then I would just submit to that plan and walk where He showed me, and do what He asked me to do. There is great value to be found in just serving Him, wherever you find yourself. Wayne and I were asked to go to Tauranga with four others and establish a Youth for Christ centre there, so we went with a resounding 'yes' to God in our hearts. I can't say I had an overwhelming passion and desire for youth work, but I did love people. So we ran youth clubs, discipled teenagers, put on monthly evangelistic concerts, and ran events - pretty much a replica of the system that I had been discipled through with Youth for Christ in Wellington. But, more than anything, we learnt what it meant to work hard and serve, regardless of what we felt our areas of gifting, and therefore perceived usefulness, were. In a nutshell, we basically grew up.

There's a simple, yet profound little devotional book that I have used nearly every day for many years called 'My Utmost for His

Highest', by Oswald Chambers. Even as I was in the process of writing this chapter, I read an excerpt that totally summed up this concept of the call of God on our lives:

"When we speak of the call of God, we are apt to forget the most important feature: the nature of the One who calls... The call is the expression of the nature from which it comes, and we can only record the call if the same nature is in us... It is the threading of God's voice to us in some particular matter and it is no use consulting anyone else about it. We have to keep that profound relationship between our souls and God. The call of God is not the echo of my nature; my affinities and personal temperament are not considered. As long as I consider my personal temperament and think about what I am fitted for, I shall never hear the call of God. But when I am brought into relationship with God, I am in the condition Isaiah was in. Isaiah's soul was so attuned to God by the tremendous crisis he had gone through that he recorded the call of God to his amazed soul. The majority of us have no ear for anything but ourselves, we cannot hear a thing God says. To be brought into the zone of the call of God, is to be profoundly altered."[2]

Through a process of stripping away my desires, God had profoundly altered me.

All the way through this journey I was still singing in church, in bands and in outreach rallies, which was possibly the strangest yet freeing thing for me. Though the dream had died, nothing had changed in the physical outworking. I just no longer had any drive or desire for it personally, and it no longer gave me any selfish joy, fulfilment or worth. How kind God is, because, through that journey which I really had no control over, everything about my heart and motivation changed. I just wanted more of Him, and loved serving Him. And, from the death of that dream, God birthed in me a greater hunger and desire for worship - my 'home'. I'm so thankful. He knew all along…

"God of my rescue, my hope's found in Christ alone
God of my rescue, my life's found in Christ, my home."

The four years in Tauranga were a huge stepping-stone in my walk with God - in the natural, Wayne and I started dating and got married while we were there. We, along with the rest of the team, worked our fingers to the bone, financially supporting both ourselves and the whole ministry. We had the privilege of discipling young people, and we forged life-long friendships. But in the spiritual, we found ourselves set on a life-path that was all about love relationship with God, and nothing less than unwavering devotion to His call and His plan, not our own!

Chapter Three
Deeper

"Lord, I want to touch Your heart
No longer standing on the outside, looking in
Lord, I want to see Your smile
And know it's there because I'm pleasing You
Deeper, Lord
To the place where it can just be me and You
Closer, Lord
I want to find Your heart and lose myself in You"

— 'Deeper'[1]

We were made for relationship with God. If our main aim in life is to get as close to the heart of our Father as possible, and walk with Him, we will have fulfilled our calling, and lived a purpose-filled life. Because everything we then DO FOR Him, flows from that heart of relationship WITH Him.

However, it is possible to be saved, yet not live the fullness of your salvation on earth. Many call Jesus Saviour, but not so many call Him Lord or Master. In other words, they accept the invitation to journey life with their Creator, but they're not so ready to let Him drive the car. It's like the hitchhiker jumping in the driver's seat, and arrogantly telling the owner of the vehicle to sit in the back. Crazy!

When someone is presented with the invitation to journey life with their Creator, they are faced with three responses. The first response, *'No'*, is a very sad one. Many people make that decision at first, whether out of fear, doubt, unbelief, or just a sheer lack of knowledge and understanding. But God is still gracious, and I believe He keeps extending the invitation until full understanding is reached.

The second response is:

"Yes, thank You, I acknowledge who You are and what You have done for me, and I would like the assurance of eternal life… but I'd still like to 'drive the car' down here."

This is the response many people unconsciously make to their Creator. This is where Jesus becomes Saviour, but not necessarily Master and Lord. Church attendance is added to their life, but usually out of duty, and compartmentalised alongside the other areas of their life. I think this response can be equally as sad as the first, because it generally amounts to a life of mixture - lived out egocentrically, yet with the convenient assurance of eternal life at the end. People who make this response are neither hot, nor cold, they are known as fence-sitters and pew-warmers, but think they're okay. They are often religious people, living out a relationship with the rules, rather than with the heart of the Father. And, therefore, the really sad thing is they have just enough knowledge of God to accept Him and feel like they've secured their destiny, but no real concept of the stunning relationship God has called them into, or the abundant and extravagant life He has for them in the here and now.

The third response is:

"Yes, thank you, I acknowledge who You are and what You have done for me, and I want to give you my life fully in return. My life is not my own… I am Yours!"

And what a ride that decision takes you on. It's obviously a lifelong journey where we make that decision over and over, as we get to know Him better, and are exposed to more of His nature and greatness. But at the outset, it's an open invitation for the Creator of the Universe to take over and turn our world upside down.

Watch what you sing...

A few years ago, Wayne and I were working with a church music team in another city in New Zealand, and we were all staying at a campsite way out in the country. This team was full of passionate young people, on fire for God, wanting to change their world. One evening we all watched the Louie Giglio DVD, 'Indescribable'[2], and then we went into a time of worship. You can imagine the atmosphere - lights were right down, and everyone's hearts were open to the bigness and awesomeness of God. There was a sense of anticipation and an expectation that we were going to worship Holy God and be encountered by Him in return. As the worship went a little deeper, people were on their knees, some were crying, and a slow refrain, *"More of You! More of You!"* started to rise. People picked up on the phrase until the whole room of people was singing it in a heartfelt and passionate way. And it was at that moment, that I felt God say to me, almost with a smile on His face:

"Do they really know what they're singing?"

It sounded like a noble thing to sing, it was definitely what they were feeling, and I'm not, in any way, suggesting it wasn't genuine, because you could feel the integrity in their hearts. But it was a dangerous thing to sing, too. I mean, what does 'more of You' really look like? None of us are really genuinely going to sing:

"I'd like juuuuust a little bit more of You Lord, but not too much. I don't want to get crazy with this!"

No, when we are caught up in the atmosphere of worship, sensing His beautiful presence, and then we sing or pray something like 'more of You!' we MEAN it at the time. It's just later on that we realise, with a gulp, that we have just invited the Creator of the Universe, the Creator of EVERYTHING in existence, to come and invade our world. And turn it upside down. None of us are really big enough to hold more of God, so in singing that song what we're really saying is:

"God I give you permission to stretch me, grow me, empty me out, and then move on in!"

But let me backtrack on my journey a little...

Faith in the face of fear...

The year after we left Tauranga Youth for Christ, Wayne and I were asked to lead another touring Y-one team called Te Haerenga Toa, which was aimed at reaching Maori and Polynesian young people. In order to do this, Wayne knew he needed to be able to speak fluently in his native tongue, Te Reo Maori, so we returned to his hometown, Whanganui, to spend a year immersed in learning. Wayne's father was a chiefly orator, a man eloquent in both the English language and Te Reo Maori but, sadly, he passed away only four weeks after we were married. The tragedy was, in wanting his sons to succeed in the 'pakeha' (white, european) world, he never taught them to speak their own language, and all his knowledge went with him to the grave. In Maori culture, the understanding is that you learn to speak at 'home' and with family, so we spent this one year in Whanganui, so Wayne could learn Te Reo under his uncle's tutelage.

This was another year of huge stretch and challenge for me, as I found myself thrust headlong into all things Maori, and, while there are some absolutely beautiful aspects to Maori culture, there can also be a huge amount of spiritual undercurrent that can go along with it. I had to learn to stand on my own two feet in the face of huge spiritual oppression, and there were times throughout that year that I felt under such oppressive attack and fear, that I felt it would break me spiritually and emotionally. God used that year to teach me to stand on faith, not feelings, especially in the light of lies the enemy tried to throw at me. And, with the press of this spiritual climate around me, the result was an even greater faith, and strengthening resolve to follow God and His way, no matter the circumstance or situation or how I felt within it.

The following year we toured New Zealand, with the Maori Y-one team. The oppressive atmosphere I had felt the year before, lifted as quickly as it had settled, and this was another incredible year of ministry and growth in a different way. We were a smaller team, performing in intermediate and secondary schools, with a higher Maori/Polynesian ratio, and doing programmes in churches and on marae (Maori Communities), as well as a big night concert in each town we visited.

Woken up...

At the beginning of that year, I had made a key decision to really commit to a greater depth and discipline in my devotional life, having quiet times with Jesus each morning, regardless of how tired I was, or what time I needed to be up in the morning. We had been on tour for a number of weeks and had arrived in Auckland - the biggest week of our touring schedule. After one particularly long day of back to back performances in Auckland secondary schools, I was physically exhausted, but, because I had formed a habit, I set my alarm for 6.00am before I went to sleep, so I could have my time with Jesus the next morning.

Well, I fell quickly into a deep, dreamless sleep but woke up the next morning at 5.00am - an hour before my alarm was due to go off. This didn't make any sense to me as I was tired, and I never usually woke up before my alarm. I got up anyway, and as I made my way to the bathroom, I asked myself out loud:

"What on earth am I doing awake?"

Immediately, and crystal clear, my question was answered, but not by me. I heard Him say, gently but almost excitably:

"I was so looking forward to our time together this morning, that I couldn't wait for your alarm to go off, so I woke you up an hour early!"

God, the Creator of THE UNIVERSE was excited about spending time with ME... and He woke me up especially to let me know that. I had CHOSEN to form a habit of daily devotion - intentionally spending time with Him no matter what - and He responded with excitement and anticipated pleasure! There have been times I have shared this story and felt almost embarrassed at what people might think - wondering if they would think I had made it up, or was being a little too 'floaty' and spiritual. But, as I mentioned, over the years I have learnt to recognise the way God speaks to me, and this was definitely Him. It was one of the most beautiful and intimate things I had ever heard Him speak to me, and you can imagine how I floated through that day. The knowledge of God's heart towards me fuelled my whole day. I was like a little lovesick puppy, wrapped up in the warmth and softness of His words to me. To be honest, this was the way we were all designed to live: resting in, and strengthened by, an intimate, personal relationship with Him - yet, we so readily allow other things to crowd out that time and steal our ease in God's presence. How incredible that we have the ability to move His heart and cause Him to draw close. Sadly, we also have the ability to hurt His heart by not drawing close to Him intentionally.

Ministry at the heart...

Wayne and I met while in ministry and have been in ministry ever since - from our days in Youth for Christ, to helping establish Excel School of Performing Arts, to touring with the Parachute Band, and now to being itinerant ministers and pastors on the staff of Equippers Church in Auckland. As part of our role at Equippers, we have had the privilege of launching Equippers Creative Lab - a full time Creative Arts School, with a large emphasis on mentoring and discipling creative hearts! What an incredible journey these years have been together! Our heart for God and His purposes, was one of the greatest things that attracted us to each other. That, and the fact that I thought he was really cute. We have walked through failure, made some pretty monumental mistakes along the way, and we know what it is to walk in God's grace, growing through some hard lessons (that may just be subject for another book!), but through it all we've always had that 'yes' in our spirits when it comes to the call of God on our lives. We got married while in full-time ministry, not caring about money, or careers, or 'the stuff' of life. And in the midst of those early ministry years, we had our two children, Gracie and Josh.

Towards the end of 1994, when Gracie was only a few months old, Wayne and I got involved with a group of musicians who had a heart for the New Zealand Christian music scene and worship, and, ironically, they were a lot of the same people that I had been involved with in Wellington Youth for Christ in my teenage years. As a 'band' we would help lead worship at Parachute Music Festival, back artists when they came over to perform and tour, and help with different artists' recording projects. I remember dragging little 7 month old Gracie around in a stroller at Parachute Festival 1995, while singing backing vocals, and having friends from church look after her while we were on stage. So the experience of ministry life started young for her! Then, at the end of 1996, Wayne was asked to produce an album of New Zealand written praise and worship songs, and we recorded it with this same group of musicians and singers. In our minds this was just a collection of New Zealand praise and worship songs - a resource for the New Zealand Church, if you like. But when 'You Alone'³ was released to New Zealand radio, and they asked who the artist was, they were informed we were just 'the band that played at Parachute Festival'. And so 'The Parachute Band' was officially birthed!

A simple 'yes'...

When I was six months pregnant with Josh (ministry life started even younger for him!), we were invited to play two songs from this first album, at Hillsong Conference in Sydney. The album found its' way into the hands of an American producer, and the demand for touring began. So Josh had his first birthday in a motel in Christchurch, while on a nationwide tour, and his second birthday in someone's home in Perth, Australia, on our first international tour. After that first international tour, the greater demand for touring in the United States began, and God provided us with an incredible nanny, so Gracie and Josh were able to stay settled at home while we toured. I had no idea God had all this in store for us... we had simply said 'yes' to whatever He might lead us into. And all this was developing as we were young parents - not an ideal time in the natural, but we have learned that God doesn't always wait for the ideal and convenient time and circumstance - otherwise, how would the challenge and stretch grow us? In fact, in hindsight, I have realised that God seems to hang His greatest miracles on the 'coathook' of our discomfort and inconvenience - nothing truly miraculous happens in the comfortable and convenient places in our lives!

The reason I mention ministry in the early parent years, is because I believe there is a real grace on young mums juggling baby and toddler routines, and the all-consuming job that is. Young mums who are sometimes working, or, as in my case, in ministry, while at the same time trying to keep their devotional life with God intact. For me it was often a case of 'grab-it-when-you-can' time with God. But there did come a time, when my kids had just grown that little bit older, that I was able to establish that daily quiet time habit again...

Tricky God...

So, fast forward a couple of years, and this is where this story picks up again. We were on tour, in Seattle, with the Parachute Band, and I had made a decision, again, to really re-establish that habit of daily quiet times with God. It's not like I hadn't been spending time with Him, but this was an intentional decision to really frame every day with that depth of devotion again. And what followed was a few months of delicious intimacy with Him, where I would read things in the Word and they would seem brand new - I would hear Him speaking to me, and it felt like this amazing sense of connection that was a whole new level for me.

One of the things I absolutely LOVE about God is the way He seems to woo and almost trick us into deeper intimacy with Him. He is so in love with us - His creation - and He longs for that love to be reciprocated. So, He takes us on this journey where we think we've made a grand decision to follow, and to press in, and to go deeper with Him. We think WE are pursuing Him, but actually, He's been pursuing us relentlessly, wooing and drawing us close, and we just don't see it until after the fact. It's like the greatest divine set up. How beautiful is that?

The Bible says that as we draw near to Him, He WILL draw near to us. We can read that as if it's we who initiate the relationship, but to me it looks like a never ending circle - we seemingly initiate, but He had already drawn us to a knowledge of Him in the first place (*'You didn't choose me, I chose you!'*), and it just keeps going round and round. And then in the midst of this open heart, intimate communication with Him, we boldly and full-of-faith pray something, or say something, or sing something, that gives Him an open invitation to take us deeper. Something like *'More of You'*, or *'Make me like You'*, or *'I just want to reflect Jesus'*... and it's like He's just been waiting for the invitation...

And that's where the journey heads into unchartered territory. All I can say is: be careful what you pray...

"Deeper Lord, to the place where it can just be me and You
Closer Lord, I want to find Your heart and lose myself in You"

I just want to reflect Jesus…

So, I was in our hotel room in Seattle, and I sat down to have my quiet time. I had been praying and thinking about my role in the Parachute Band and the fact that I was leading worship, sometimes in front of thousands of people, in big churches in America, and I didn't want to ever have attention drawn to me, but just wanted people to see Jesus when I led. And I found myself praying one of THOSE prayers: *"I just want to reflect Jesus… I just want to reflect Jesus… I JUST WANT TO REFLECT JESUS!"* It was a heartfelt and genuine prayer… and God heard it…

…and He'd been waiting for it.

My daily habit was to read a Psalm, and then the chapter of Proverbs that corresponded with the day's date. There was always something good to be found in Proverbs. However, this day, I got the date wrong - I thought it was February 27th (which was a little ironic since it was actually Wayne's birthday, the 26th, and I KNEW that). But I have learned there is no such thing as a coincidence with God, and I launched into reading Proverbs 27. Hindsight would show me, it may have been the wrong date, but it was the right proverb!

The first thing I read was Proverbs 27:19:

"As a face is reflected in water, so the heart reflects the real person." (NLT)[4]

My initial response was:

"Cool! God is speaking to me! I've just prayed about wanting to reflect Jesus, and He's shown me a verse about water reflecting the face, and a man's heart reflecting the real person. It all ties in - He's even used the same words!"

This was going to be a gooooood quiet time! But as I thought about it some more, I started to feel slightly uncomfortable. Wait, *"... the heart reflects the real person"?* Hmmmm... I knew what was in my heart, in the deepest places that no-one else saw, and it wasn't always pretty.

I pushed that feeling aside, and decided to keep reading. Surely after months of delicious intimacy, where I felt like the 'Golden Child' in His presence, God wasn't going to ruin it by challenging me?

The next verse that jumped off the page at me was this one, Proverbs 27:21:

"As the crucible is for silver and the furnace is for gold, so a person is proved by the praise he receives." (NET)[5]

I really didn't care for THAT one very much. Crucibles and furnaces did not sound very pleasant at all. Why was God showing me this? I had just prayed a noble prayer: *"I just want to reflect Jesus"*, and He was showing me verses about my heart being the true reflection of who I am, and silver in crucibles and gold in furnaces, which all sounded rather hot and uncomfortable.

This quiet time was not feeling quite so gooooood anymore...

So I decided to flick to the New Testament and find something lovely to read about God's unconditional love, or His grace being sufficient, or something of that nature. My Bible stopped just short of the New Testament, at Malachi 3.

My first reaction was: *"Yesss, I'm safe! It's just the tithing chapter!"*

Clearly, I had not read Malachi 3 in its entirety before because, as I scanned the page, my eyes fell on verses 2-4, and my heart sank as I read this:

"For He will be like a refiner's fire or a launderer's soap. He will sit as a refiner and purifier of silver: He will purify the Levites and refine them like gold and silver. Then the Lord will have men who will bring offerings in righteousness, and the offerings of Judah and Jerusalem

will be acceptable to the Lord, as in days gone by, as in former years." (NIV)[6]

This was just too close for comfort, and too uncanny to be coincidence. I had prayed, *"I just want to reflect Jesus,"* and God was clearly showing me that there was some heart surgery required in order to make that possible. After these few months of amazing intimacy, where I thought I had fully arrived in my relationship with God, He was talking to me about the depths of my heart, that no-one else really saw, and this seemed to be inextricably linked with the crucible and the refiner's fire. You have to understand, I loved Jesus with all my heart, and I wanted to live right and to honour and glorify Him, but I had come to a crossroads in the journey and, with the utterance of that honest prayer, I had unwittingly given God permission to move on in and turn on the spotlight.

And immediately, almost audibly, I heard Him say,

"You're going in the fire."

Well, to say I was thrilled to hear Him speak to me SOOOO clearly, would not be completely honest, in fact my first response was, *"Oh dang it..."* but at the same time there was a flicker of excitement that if God had spoken it, He'd be in control of it, and He's likely more sure of what He's doing than I am. Deep down, too, I think I was probably a little sick of this grunge that I knew was slopping around in the recesses of my heart.

And then I read the passage that brought this thing full circle. I was using the NIV Worship Bible, at the time, and each page had little excerpts and thoughts in the margins, written by people who were well known in worship circles worldwide. Some were poems or prayers, and others were commentary on certain verses. And wouldn't you know it, OF COURSE, there was a little explanation of Malachi 3:2-4 written in the margin:

"Our Father, who seeks to perfect His saints in holiness, knows the value of the refiner's fire. It is with the most precious metals that the assayer takes the most pains, and subjects them to the hot fire, because such fires melt the metal, and only the molten mass releases its alloy or takes perfectly its new form in the mold. The old refiner NEVER leaves His crucible, but sits down by it lest there should be one excessive degree of heat to mar the metal. But as soon as he skims from the surface the last of the dross, and **SEES HIS OWN FACE REFLECTED**, he puts out the fire."[7]

I could hardly believe my eyes! I had started this quiet time with an honest prayer, *"I just want to reflect Jesus,"* and God had rushed in, with my open invitation, to show me His process - the only way this could be achieved.

"You say you want to reflect Jesus? Well your heart has some stuff in it which is incompatible at the moment with His image, but because I love you so much, and I want greater intimacy in our relationship, I'm going to put the metal of your life in a crucible, heat up the fire underneath it, and cause that stuff to come to the surface, so I can skim it off and throw it away. And as the metal of your heart becomes more pure, I will at last see My face reflected in it, and then I'll put the fire out!"

This was not a process of discipline as I at first thought. This was a process of love! A process of intimacy! What He was actually saying to me was:

"Your life is precious to Me. Our love relationship is precious to Me, and your desire to reflect My Son, pleases Me greatly. And because I want a greater level of intimacy with you, I will not leave your heart untouched and unrefined. You have given Me permission, now I will go to work! But I am the silversmith, and I WILL sit close through the whole process. I won't leave you. I know how hot the fire needs to be to begin and complete this process, and I will be in control of it. I won't let it ruin the metal of your heart because it is PRE-CIOUS to Me."

NOT a bed of roses...

From the moment I finished that quiet time, I knew I was in the fire. I didn't have to do anything to start the process, and I could do nothing to get myself out of it, so I can't even explain to you what happened. But I knew it was God and He was in control.

And it was HORRIBLE...

Almost immediately, things started coming up from the depths of my heart to the surface of my consciousness. Attitudes that I hid from others because they weren't the sorts of attitudes a Christian, no less a worship-leader should have. Obviously, along with that, was the fear that if I showed these things to people, they would not accept me, or worse, reject me, based on who I really was. So I had hidden them away. How easy it is to wear a facade, yet be completely unaware that we are! Then there were reactions and responses to Wayne and my kids that were just plain selfish and self-centred. They were ugly and wrong, and I knew it, but I could no longer control them and push them away, as up they came to the surface. I think I must have been hell to live with in the midst of this process.

Then God started working on my comparisons and jealousy towards other females. And insecurity and low self-esteem from my early teenage years. Yep, they were all still there too - things I thought had been dealt with long ago - but their roots were still tangled in my heart, and they had to go. Judgemental attitudes, criticism, control and self-righteousness were a few of the juicy little 'delights' that came up.

I can remember one day sitting down to have my quiet time, and feeling such a sense of self-loathing at what I was seeing in my own heart. Here I was leading worship in an international touring band, supposedly the example of what a 'good Christian' should look like, yet feeling like I was the worst person in the world, and I thought everyone could see it. But, with that honest assessment, came the desire for God to just deal with it all, once and for all.

And as I came face-to-face with the grime and filth of my humanity, I would cry out to God, *"I hate this stuff, I hate who I am!"* And He, the Silversmith, would skim off the muck, and I would hear Him tenderly say, *"Oh, but I love you! I adore you, just as you are, right now. Not as you think you need to be in order to earn my love!"* That's a miracle right there! No other human could truly give that sort of unconditional love, in the midst of our shame, and the depths of our rotten, honest and most vulnerable humanity. This was probably the beginning of the connection between God's love for me and my love for myself. And it was the most healing thing - the beginning of me really understanding what His unconditional love really looked like. Love that was too great to allow me to stay the way I was. And I began to feel more free. Especially as I stopped striving and simply surrendered and rested in the process, knowing that He was in control of it. And I felt safe in His saving arms...

Fire is attractive...

A few years ago, Wayne and the kids and I had a holiday at Pukehina Beach, in the Bay of Plenty. It was Easter, so summer had well and truly ended, and, although the autumn days were still quite balmy and warm, the evenings held a lovely crisp chill. A few of these evenings we wrapped up warmly and lit a bonfire on the beach to cook sausages and toast marshmallows. And I remember sitting, huddled together by the fire, appreciating its warmth, but mostly just being still and watching it burn. There's something about fire that attracts us to it, whether in a hearth, or an open bonfire. The dance of the flames is mesmerising and mysterious...

As is God's process with the crucible and the fire. One of the most remarkable things to me, in the hottest part of this refining journey, was that people would come up to me and say, *"What is God doing in you right now? I can see Him all over you!"* and my inner, incredulous response was, *"Hah! If only you knew!"* I found it so hard to believe that people were seeing God in me when all I was seeing was my ugly humanity. Ah, but isn't that just the way of God? When He is in control of a situation, when we surrender to the process and just let Him do what He needs to do, and when we are truly aware of the freedom of His unconditional love, people begin to see more of Him and less of us…

Chapter Four
God Knows What He's Up To!

"There's a place, where freedom reigns
 Great exchange was made for me
 From hidden shame, to life in You
 My heart awakened
As I draw near You see me, Your love it runs to meet me
 Your grace, it covers me
And Your love, it washes me
Surely mercy will follow me
Always, always
    Take me back to the Cross
    Take me back to the Cross"

- 'Grace'[1]

One of the greatest areas that God needed to address in the crucible, was my unhealthy self-image. I mentioned in an earlier chapter that, as a teenager, based largely on some words spoken to me when I was younger, I really struggled with low self-esteem and bad self-image. I understood in my head that God loved me, but I could not love myself. And even with God's love, it can be a long journey from the head to the heart, and this process was a big part of that journey. God had dealt with the singing issue, and the worth I gained from that, but that was reasonably surface level stuff, and the much more deeply rooted issue behind why I needed that worth from something I could do, remained unchecked for the longest time. This has been a huge life challenge to this point.

There were different times when I knew parts of this issue were highlighted and dealt with, but it took the heat of the fire to bring the magnitude of it to light. This thing was like an emotional cancer - it affected the way I thought and felt about myself, and it skewed my perception of God's love. As I said, I had no trouble accepting God's love based on His nature, as long as that love was independent of me. But believing that God loved me because I was love-worthy and He really LIKED me, was much harder to accept. It also affected the way I felt about my marriage - deep down in places I didn't even recognise at the time - I actually believed that Wayne married me only because it was God's will, not because he really loved me, almost like he was spiritually forced to. But it also took me down a very dangerous and dark path when it came to my external image.

Don't judge a book by its cover...

When I was a young thing, I was affectionately nick-named 'Puff' because I was a 'healthily proportioned' baby, and, apparently, I would stop every few steps while learning to walk, and pant, somewhat out of breath. I was unaware of this obviously, but as I grew through my primary years, and that gnawing feeling of loneliness, and being out of place also grew, I clung to whatever I could to find my worth, and where I belonged. Because I felt unacceptable, the need for people's acceptance was hugely important to me. In hindsight as an adult, I have also learned that my primary love language is 'words of affirmation', so as a young one, when words were spoken that I perceived as a rejection of me as a person, they created a space of lack and need within me.

As a teenager, I would swing between looking healthy and being a little overweight, and I felt the constant need and pressure to be working on my weight. I would try fad diets and exercise, believing the next eating plan would be my answer to internal happiness, so warped was my opinion of myself, and my belief that people's opinion of me was largely tied up in my physical appearance. Worse than that, was the belief that I was not a worthwhile person if I was overweight - this is how deeply the negative words innocently spoken to me when I was younger, by someone outside of my immediate family, had been driven. A lie had been sown, and a deep sense of shame about my image, had taken up residence in my spirit at that point. I didn't consciously think these things; the thought processes were so deeply rooted that the attitudes and behaviours that followed, came from an unconscious place emotionally. Those thought processes, and the unbearable feelings they created, affected me, and undergirded everything about me, well into my adult years. Like I said earlier, what a huge waste of time and energy it was, being so self-centred and obsessed.

Misguided honour...

But alongside the unhealthy desire to be thin, was a very normal desire to be healthy! And I subtly switched my focus and motivation for being thin, to being healthy and honouring God. After all, I was in a visual, public ministry on the platform, where I was constantly being looked at, and looked to, as an example. Besides, I told myself that being thin and fit would give me greater stamina with touring and performing. The crazy thing is, this is all true, but the motivation behind it was all so wrong and twisted, and I justified the life out of that thing, until I actually believed my motivation was pure.

Believing I was doing the right thing, and honouring God by being 'healthy', I started using an eating plan which involved counting points assigned to different types of foods, that helped me to lose weight in a controlled and balanced way. I need to stress, that for anyone who doesn't have an emotional and addictive connection to their image, and uses wisdom, it is actually a fantastic tool that works, and has given a lot of people real freedom. But for me, whose happiness, worth and security was directly linked to my physical image and my ability to control that, it was extremely unhealthy. Rather than use the system to bring freedom and enjoy the journey, I became obsessed with counting the points. I was allocated a total number of points per day, but I would add up fractions of a point, and journal every little thing I ate. And if I was half a point over my allowance on any given day,

I would feel like a failure, and it would drive me crazy inside. I would also weigh myself. Not once a week, to healthily mark and measure progress, but eight or nine times A DAY! This was how grossly unhealthy my thoughts were about my external image.

Added to that was the exercise - I would exercise like a crazy woman. Again, I believed it was for the honour and glory of God to keep myself fit, but my hidden motivation was driven by my emotional deficit. Along with the points counting, I would exercise every day, and if something happened in a day that upset my plans to exercise, I would feel very agitated and irritable inside. I COULD NOT LOSE CONTROL OF THIS. This was my freedom, this was my worth, this was for God's glory! That was the self-talk that unconsciously sprung from my thinking. But the very thing I thought was going to bring me security, self-worth and freedom, was actually imprisoning and chaining me up in my soul and spirit.

And it was becoming an idol to me…

In the midst of all this obsessive exercising and dieting, I became extremely judgemental and critical of others whom I did not perceive to be as disciplined as I was, and clearly did not feel it important to honour God with a healthy lifestyle. I was religious to a fault - I can tell you, it was not an attractive trait. But I felt I needed to help them see the light so I would 'encourage' them to get fit and healthy. Really I was trying to control them because of my own lack of freedom, and one day, when Wayne said to me, *"You were a much nicer person when you were bigger!"* I was absolutely shocked… there was not a hint of malice behind his statement, just pure truth, and I needed to hear it.

God wasn't buying it…

Clearly, God didn't think I was bringing Him ANY glory, or making Him look any better, and graciously He had a plan.

Remember, this was all part of the fire journey, so I was still having my quiet times, and pressing into Him, and loving Him with all my heart, and I was COMPLETELY genuine and heartfelt in my pursuit of His heart. But there's only so long you can journey, holding the reins and trying to keep everything under wraps, before God says, *"It's my turn to take over - this thing is destroying you!"* God is so good like that, and I'm so very thankful.

In my experience, God never just storms in and turns everything upside down without preparing you first. But it's nearly always only hindsight that reveals that preparation. He graciously and kindly leads you to understanding, and then, when your heart is open, He starts to touch on the issues. And with the help of Wayne, and some other caring friends who were bold and kind enough to question me, my health, and my motivation, He was starting to do that.

We were on holiday, staying at a friend's place in Tauranga and I had my 'points' book with me so I could keep track of every single little morsel that passed my lips. But one morning, after my quiet time, I felt God very clearly say to me:

"Rip up the book and throw it away."

I have enough fear of the Lord to know that it's best to do what He says, and, before I could question whether it really was Him speaking, I went ahead and did it. I was not prepared for the emotional upheaval that followed and, as I threw the torn-up book into the rubbish bin, I flew into absolute panic mode.

"How will I know the points value of every thing I eat?"
"How will I keep a track of what I'm eating?"
"What if I get it wrong and overeat?"
"What if I get really fat?"

But my biggest scream inside was still:

"I CAN'T LOSE CONTROL OF THIS!"

There was so much fear associated with it. I didn't want to get fat. I didn't want to feel bad about myself. I didn't want to dishonour God! And they were all soul-ish lies! It got to the point where I was so distraught, that I was laying on the floor, almost in the foetal position, stressed out and crying like a baby, while Wayne prayed for me and probably thought, *"Who on earth is this woman, and what has she done with my wife?"*

I jest now, but at the time it was so real and actually so very frightening - the extent of my emotions wrapped up in this horrible thing, was terrifying. The next day, after I had calmed down, I thought to myself, *"Well, at least I can still exercise!"* So, even though I was no longer allowed to obsess about counting my points, I decided to just increase the exercise and all would be well. And off I went for my morning power-walk, and I felt like I was back in control - I had the reins firmly in my grasp again! Peace in my heart was resumed.

But God had another surprise up His very big sleeve. That afternoon, we were at the beach, in the water playing with the kids, and as I sprung off one foot to jump a wave, I felt a tearing sensation in my Achilles tendon. Doubled over in pain and literally not able to walk, Wayne helped me out of the water and back to the beach, and we gathered our things and headed off to the Emergency Department. I had strained my Achilles and I hobbled out of there on crutches unable to bear any weight, or do any exercise whatsoever. How seriously comical is God? How very KIND is God...

Knight in shining armour...

God had to step in, in a very physical way, in order to stop me in my tracks and begin to address the heart of the matter. I don't believe I had an eating disorder, but I was so very borderline. I didn't necessarily have to be throwing up, or starving myself, yet I was grossly affected by the strength of the lies I was allowing myself to believe, and the root issue was the same. In fact, I believe there are many, many people who are caught in the grip of this horrible mental battle like I was, but no-one really knows, sees or understands the hold it has on them. And because they aren't necessarily diagnosed as bulimic or anorexic, they minimise their situation by saying they have it under control and don't have a problem. My physical outworking of this was merely symptomatic of what was going on underneath emotionally - my need to control and make myself feel better about myself. My obsession was nothing short of idolatry and God HAD to address that. So He took me on a journey where He began to really address those root issues - again, so much of it was healed in the knowledge, revelation and application of His perfect, unconditional love for me - my knight in shining armour! And then I needed to learn to walk that out by disciplining my thoughts, emotions and speech, which I'm going to chat to you about in another chapter.

You see, we can tackle external symptoms in any area of our lives, but, unless the root emotional issue is dealt with, nothing will change. There is little point in dealing with the effect if we haven't identified and addressed the cause! Trying to do that leads to BONDAGE, and RELIGIOUS behaviour. Doing things to appease God, and make ourselves feel worthwhile and worth something. I desperately wanted to live in FREEDOM and RELATIONSHIP, and nothing less than the Blood of Jesus and His unconditional love, poured out on the Cross, could do that for me.

"I am no longer driven to impress God. Christ lives in me. The life you see me living is not "mine", but it is lived by faith in the Son of God, who loved me and gave Himself for me. I am not going to go back on that! Is it not clear to you that to go back to that old rule-keeping, peer-pleasing religion would be an abandonment of everything personal and free in my relationship with God? I refuse to do that, to repudiate God's grace. If a living relationship with God could come by rule-keeping, then Christ died unnecessarily!" (Galations 2:20-21 MSG)

"Your grace, it covers me
Your love, it washes me
Surely mercy will follow me
Always, always
Take me back, to the Cross
Take me back, to the Cross"

I choose freedom...

I choose to live in the freedom Jesus' blood afforded me at the Cross. Nothing else can truly set me free. The Bible says that He has made forever perfect, all those whom He is making holy. To me, that verse is one of the most comforting verses in Scripture. It means that our spirit is perfect, blameless in the sight of God, because of the righteousness and Blood of Jesus, but our soul is walking the journey to holiness and wholeness. We were saved in an instant, but we're being saved on the journey of a lifetime. This fire-journey wasn't a quick fix, overnight thing. If I'm really honest with you, there are still many aspects of my life that God is still working on in the fire, and definitely will be until the day I get to see my Saviour face to face. But I'm so thankful that God's love is not candy floss, or sugar sweet, but it's strong and gutsy enough to not leave us where we are, but to graciously mould, shape and change us. And the journey is so truly worth it.

Chapter Five
How Can I Not Sing?

"Holy, holy is Your Name, God Almighty
Worthy, worthy of all praise
Now I'm standing face to face
With the God of grace and mercy
And the One who took my place, set me free
     Jesus, You're worthy, Jesus You're worthy
     Jesus, You're worthy of all praise
How can I not sing? Freedom came to earth to rescue me
How can I not sing? Glory came to earth to set me free... so I sing!"
-'Worthy'[1]

"Long before He laid down earth's foundations, He had us in mind, had settled on us as the focus of His love, to be made whole and holy by His love. Long, long ago He decided to adopt us into His family through Jesus Christ. He wanted us to enter into the celebration of His lavish gift-giving by the hand of His beloved Son. Because of the sacrifice of the Messiah, His blood poured out on the altar of the Cross, we're a free people – free of penalties and punishments chalked up by all our misdeeds. And not just barely free, either. ABUNDANTLY free!" (Ephesians 1:3-7 MSG)

What an absolute wonder, a mystery that is difficult to truly fathom, that long **before** He laid down earth's foundations, God saw us. He had already decided we were the object of His affection, adoption papers had been drawn up and signed, we were His children. That was the plan from the beginning. God the Father, with a multitude of children, living in love relationship with Him. But God didn't just want children who would love Him out of duty, He wanted us to have the choice – the freedom to choose Him. That meant He chose risk - the chance that we would reject Him. So from the moment that freedom was first exercised, and sin entered the world, the Father has been relentlessly pursuing the heart of His children to win us back!

The Bible says in 1 Corinthians 6:12:

"Just because something is technically legal doesn't mean that it is spiritually appropriate. If I went around doing whatever I thought I could get by with, I'd be a slave to my whims." (MSG)

Many people think freedom means the removal of all restrictions, limitations and boundaries. The ability to choose to do whatever I want, whenever I want, with no fear of consequences, either to myself or to others around me. They think that would be heaven, but personally, that sounds more like hell to me. And where there is no relationship important or precious enough to hold a person's heart and devotion - where self is elevated above God and above others - this sort of 'freedom' will only bind, confine, and chain the human soul with shackles that cannot be seen.

I think you know what I'm going to say next… it's the thread that has been running through this entire book so far. You and I were designed for the freedom that is established and grounded in a living, vital, growing and intimate relationship with our Creator. It completely blows me away that, while we were still sinners, lost and far away from God, and caught up in our hopeless, pointless lives, Jesus had already died for us to make it possible to have relationship with our Father again. What enormous love, what enormous passion. And what we once perceived, in our lost state, as the chains of restraint, we now see as the foundation of FREEDOM. A relationship with our Creator, in which, because of grace, it is a joyous thing to say, *"Not my will, but yours!"* That is true freedom.

And yes, it really is that simple. If all God longs for is the re-establishment of connection and relationship with His children, surely it makes sense that He's not going to make it hard for us to find the way back to Him? I'm not saying that Jesus' death on the Cross was easy for Him or for His Father - anything but - but His death and resurrection, God's grace, love and mercy poured out at the Cross, made it easy for us. Just accept the invitation...

Wired for freedom...

FREEDOM! It is one of the most delicious words to me. As I explained at the beginning of this book, even though I was basically living a good life, even at the age of 12, I KNEW I wasn't free. But I saw that freedom in my sister, and I hungered and yearned for it. My sin had already been dealt with on the Cross, but it wasn't until I simply accepted that, that I knew I was forgiven, and relationship with God, my Father, was restored. I was instantly changed. And I was instantly FREE!

It's all in the wiring...

We were wired for freedom. We were set free, so we could LIVE free. And not just a little bit free, but madly, wildly, contagiously free! That's what our souls respond to, that's how we operate best, and that's what will model freedom to the world around us. The overriding problem seems to be that we say we're free, we like to think we're free, but the majority of us aren't really LIVING in that freedom. A bird that has had its wings clipped, or is living in a cage, is still **being** what it was designed to **be**, but it's not **doing** what it was designed to **do**, which is to fly. A dog chained in a yard may be able to run in circles, believing it's free, but, in the end, it is still chained, being a dog but not being able to do what it's wired to do, which is run free. What good are we to the world around us, if we declare freedom in Jesus, yet we're still walking around chained ourselves, bowed down under the weight of guilt, condemnation, sin and addictive or compulsive behaviours? The world looks on and sees someone who is no better off than they are, or sometimes in a worse state, and their response is likely, *"You can keep your freedom in Jesus, if THAT'S what it looks like!"*

Now you know I'm not talking about putting on a facade and pretending we've got it all together, in order to not shame and dishonour God, because we feel we need to win the world. That sort of striving can only last so long before something has to give. Again, once we have the revelation of freedom, it is still a journey to walk that out in many different areas of our lives. And there is great power in admitting honestly and humbly that we're all 'works in progress', and that we haven't yet arrived. But the bottom line and foundation of this freedom in Christ, is that He died so you could walk free. It's independent of you and it's an irrefutable truth whether you FEEL completely free yet or not. That freedom stands regardless, which is why the Bible says:

"So if the Son liberates you [makes you free men], then you are really and unquestionably free." (John 8:36 AMP)[2]

The free spirit ...

So, of course, there's a process that is all part of this journey once we've accepted the invitation. The first thing you need to know is that the freedom you were designed for isn't achieved by your striving and personal discipline, worked out through a self-help programme. I'm all for self-discipline and growing as a person, but not if that's my recipe for freedom - that sort of striving, without knowing WHY you're free, will just bind you up in the end.

Galations 5:1-6 and 16-18 says:

"Christ has set us free to live a free life. So take your stand! Never again let anyone put a harness of slavery on you. I am emphatic about this. The moment any one of you submits to circumcision or any other rule-keeping system, at that same moment Christ's hard-won gift of freedom is squandered... when you attempt to live by your own religious plans and projects, you are cut off from Christ, you fall out of grace... My counsel is this: Live freely, animated and motivated by God's Spirit. Then you won't feed the compulsions of selfishness. For there is a root of sinful self-interest in us that is at odds with a free spirit, just as the free spirit is incompatible with selfishness... Why don't you choose to be led by the Spirit and so escape the erratic compulsions of a law-dominated existence." (MSG)

Even though we all have God's law written inherently on our hearts, God knew we were incapable of keeping the law through our own strength and determination. Once Christ went to the Cross, we were no longer tied to a system of laws, rules and regulations just for law's sake, but because of grace, God's endless favour, relationship came into effect. What the law demanded, grace fulfilled, and in response to grace, a love relationship with Jesus demands a greater level of living. And makes it possible, providing a greater level of freedom for our souls. You don't take the gift of amazing grace for granted; you guard it as precious!

There's something about a love relationship that makes you want to be your very best for that person, that wants to give to them, and make them feel adored and treasured. And when you act in selfishness, hurting them, you feel the chasm those actions create. You can feel the pain you have brought to that person's heart. I mentioned that without an important and precious relationship to hold our heart, we are prone to throwing off the perceived constraints of freedom, only to ensnare our soul. That's one of the reasons God desires an intimate relationship with us - the most important and precious of all relationships - because He knows it's good for us, and keeps our soul free. I retain my freedom when I place the constraints of a moral code around my heart. I retain my freedom when I choose NOT to do whatever I feel like, whenever I feel like it. That true freedom is good for my soul! And, let's face it, as Galations 5 says there is still that root of sinful self-interest in us that is at odds with the free spirit.

Relationship with Him will cause us to not want to hurt Him with the choices we make. Relationship with Him will keep us running back for more of Him rather than tasting the empty, tired substitutes the world has to offer. Jesus truly does become the cup that never runs dry!

Freedom in action...

In my last year at high school, I went to a few parties with my friends and had the odd drink, but I never got drunk (and to this day, never have been!) Because I knew what the Bible said about drinking - it's okay to have a drink, but getting drunk is wrong - there was a moral code written in my heart. But it was my love relationship with Jesus that really added weight to that, because I didn't want to do anything that would hurt Him, or steal the freedom of my soul.

Some would say:

"That's not freedom - that's legalistic and you're missing out on a whole lot of fun! Boring Christian following the rules!"

I would say, it's the greatest freedom there is because it's true freedom based on relationship with God's heart, NOT religious laws and rules. The foundation of love relationship with Jesus causes me to want to guard that intimacy and keep my soul free, so I willingly put those restraints around these areas.

In my 7th form year, I also had my one and only boyfriend, besides Wayne. I don't care whether you think I'm prudish or whatever, but I wish I hadn't gone down that road, but just completely waited for my husband. I was a Christian, and it seemed this guy was trying hard to be one, because he knew it was important to me. And, for the eight months we dated, I still had my quiet times, and I still went to church, and I still talked the talk - it looked like nothing had changed in my lifestyle, especially as I actually told myself that I could maybe bring him closer to Jesus.

Yet, because I knew it was a wrong relationship, the gaping distance I felt from my Jesus was like a festering sore that wouldn't heal. My love relationship with Jesus was fully compromised, because I didn't want to give my boyfriend up, and I HATED that feeling. I felt empty and desperately sad, as I had exchanged something earthly and temporal, for the richness of my love for Him. Again, it was that sense of loss that drove me back to Him, and wanting to keep my soul free, I placed the restraints of freedom around future relationships, and made a decision to not date anyone until it was my husband. It doesn't mean my emotions didn't go there a few times in between - I WAS normal - but staying free in my soul was way more important to me.

Some would say:

"That's not freedom, that's naive and immature - young people should have the freedom to have some fun before marrying one person for life. What if you decide after you're married, that you really don't love each other after all, or wish you'd had more experience? Testing the waters is all part of maturing and growing up!"

I would say, it's the greatest freedom there is, freedom that guards intimacy with Jesus first, keeping your soul free, and trusting that the Creator of the Universe cares and knows more about what your future holds, than you do. I don't mean this in any way to be a source of condemnation for those who have been in a number of relationships, just an encouragement to truly seek God and love relationship with Him, as your first source of joy and fulfilment. Doing that, will pretty much ensure that you hear His heart on your future.

Relationship with His heart...

More than anything else, after recognising and acknowledging Jesus' death on the cross for me, it has been my love relationship with Him that has continually encouraged me to keep my heart and soul free. When we have truly tasted the depths of His unconditional love and full acceptance, we are completely ruined for anything else. As I said earlier, Jesus truly does become the cup that never runs dry. And I can always sense when 'stuff' starts to clutter my soul again, and it feels ugly, so I'm quick to run back to that place of intimacy and clear it up. Soul freedom is that important to me.

Relationship with His heart is always the bottom line. If we stop doing certain things because of a fear of punishment from an angry God, or from a misguided place of self-striving and improvement, we have entered a relationship with the rules, and that will always lead to legalistic thinking and religion. I read a quote recently that said, *"Restraint without revelation, leads to rebellion."* In other words, without the personal revelation of the heart relationship, founded in complete intimacy with our Creator, we will try to adhere to rules and regulations, a list of 'do's and don'ts' to appease an angry God. And eventually that sort of living and striving leaves us bone dry and wanting to quit. But when we have a revelation that He is not angry with us, and we are actually unpunishable; when we truly realise what grace means - that Jesus cleared the debt of sin once and for all - we will celebrate in that knowledge and want to keep our hearts close.

Freedom looks good, tastes good, and carries a sweet fragrance with it. It embodies hope, life, joy, peace and love. Sin is just the opposite. And, contrary to popular opinion, sin is not the wrong stuff we DO - those things are simply the external out-workings of a sinful internal disposition. Sin, at its most basic, is separation from the heart of God. It is living outside of His heart, His way and His care, deciding our own way is best instead. And it looks bad, tastes bad, and stinks! But chase His heart, pursue Him, and the things that are near and dear to Him, and you will find your soul living in true freedom.

Chapter Six
It Begins in the Mind

"My freedom, my reason, my Saviour that's what You are to me
You free me, complete me, my Saviour that's what You are
There's no other like You, there's no-one besides You
You're more than my heart can contain
    And I will love You all my life
    For You are my Freedom, the One that I live for
    I will love You all my life
    For You are my Freedom, You're the One that I live for"
- 'All my Life'[1]

I have mentioned there are certain areas in our lives that we find freedom in straight away - a decision based on a moral code but driven by a love relationship with our Creator. Drinking, relationships, peer pressure etc, were never really huge issues for me and, therefore once the restraints of freedom were applied, my soul stayed free in those areas. However, the freedom I needed to find in the whole weight and image issue, was a much lengthier process, because the binding nature of it was rooted in something so much deeper - it had hooked me in my soul, and woven its tentacles around the very fabric of my thought processes and emotions, and these needed to be challenged and changed. Again, it was my relationship with Jesus and His unconditional love for me that healed me in that area, but the journey took a long time and, to be honest, is definitely something that I will always need to guard my thinking about.

Thorn in the flesh?

In the midst of that journey, I would read verses like, *"Christ set us free to live a free life"* and *"He who the Son sets free, is free indeed,"* yet I would feel anything BUT free in this area. And it was such a constant source of confusion for me. I wanted to believe what the Bible said, but I had more faith in my feelings when it came to this issue because they seemed so very real. I knew Jesus had died to cleanse me from sin - I had no trouble believing that - but when it came to the feelings and huge insecurity about my image and weight, was there really freedom for me in this, or was it my 'thorn in the flesh' that I just had to live with?

This is where I want to head in this chapter - the process of gaining freedom based on what we think, what we feel, and what we speak.

Plumb line of the Word...

We need to remember that the basis of our freedom is Jesus dying on the Cross for us, making way for a relationship with our Father. We can't do anything to earn our own freedom, we have no worth in and of ourselves. It's completely about Jesus' sacrifice on the cross, and, because of His death and His blood, we are completely RIGHTEOUS and free. Whether we feel like it or not, that is the absolute TRUTH. So much of what is presented to us today as truth, is man-theorised and philosophied, a little bit of the truth mixed with a whole lot of man's ideas and theories. Or situational truth, watered down, with no real grounding, and can change according to different circumstances. This is why it is vitally important to keep the truth of God's word as our plumb line. Either the Bible is completely true or it's not. If there is one little aspect of it that is not, then we cannot trust any of it as absolute truth. So, from the very start, we have to choose to believe that the Bible is the absolute Word of God. And, as we start to dwell on the truth of Scripture, we find it begins to shape and define our thinking, and therefore our reality.

So we start from this foundation:

"If you stick with this, living out what I tell you, you are my disciples for sure. Then you will experience for yourselves the truth, and the truth will set you free... So if the Son sets you free, you are free, through and through." (John 8:32, 36 MSG)

And this one:

"Thus we have been set free to experience our rightful heritage. You can tell for sure that you are now fully adopted as His own children because God sent the Spirit of His Son into our hearts crying out, "Papa! Father!" Doesn't that privilege of intimate conversation with God make it plain that you are not a slave, but a child? And if you are a child, you're also an heir, with complete access to the inheritance." (Galations 4:5-7 MSG)

What these passages are basically saying is this:

If I stick to the truth, clinging to it, and living it out as a follower of Jesus, I will experience His truth, and it will set me free. And that means free, THROUGH AND THROUGH. The reason I've been set free is to experience God's love as a child, not as a slave - that's my heritage and my inheritance. A child has rights with their father, but a slave has none. That intimate relationship is confirmed in my heart through the indwelling Holy Spirit - not through what I FEEL. So I will cling to the truth, I will stick with the truth, I will live in the truth - I am a child of God, I am free, and everything that belongs to God, belongs to me - I have complete access!

Wow... If we could just discipline ourselves to THINK that everyday, it would change EVERYTHING about the way we live.

Barricade the road...

The way we think is so very powerful. I know, for me, it's not wise to spend too much time alone with my thoughts, because, without discipline, they can start to go wayward. It is possible for me to wake up in the morning feeling great, but an hour later, I'm down in the dumps because I've thought something negative and it's shaped the way I feel. My undisciplined thoughts will define and shape my day if I'm not careful. The thing about this passage in John 8, is that it does give us an instruction - *"If you stick with this, LIVING OUT WHAT I TELL YOU, you are My disciples for sure..."* This certainly implies some EFFORT on our part. If we don't discipline our thoughts, they will begin to rule. The problem is, if they're not based in truth, they can take us down all sorts of wrong back alleys.

Psalms 119:29-30 says:

"Barricade the road that goes Nowhere; grace me with Your clear revelation. I choose the true road to Somewhere, I post your road signs at every curve and corner." (MSG)

Wrong thought patterns are like a road that goes NOWHERE, and we must be diligent to barricade that road. A barricade is designed not to be broken through - it is strong, it says 'NO ENTRY' under any circumstance. It can suggest the road is dangerous to traverse. Or it might say, 'This road is no longer an option - find another route.' WE are the ones who have to build the barricade though, God's not going to do that for us. Too often I've heard people pray that God would take their wrong thoughts away, but He has given us the tools to do that ourselves. We need to be diligent to grab our thoughts, examine them in the light of God's Word and way, and, if they don't measure up, we must throw them out. The barricade gets built through choice, determination and submission to a higher way - God's Way.

You are what you think...

In the beginning, this process takes a LOT of effort and discipline. If there has been a thought pattern that has become a stronghold in our minds, to the extent that we're not even aware of the initial wrong thought anymore, we need to ask God to help us trace it back, and rediscover the source again. Then we can dig it out and reshape our thinking with the TRUTH. My thinking about my image had become so warped - I thought I was fat and I believed the wicked lie which told me that this made me a worthless human being. Before I realised it, that thinking had become so ingrained that it was no longer a conscious thought. It was a brain-rut that had formed, and my emotions could do nothing but follow it, feel it, and live it out. My responses to many different situations always echoed that stronghold in my thinking, and it needed to be traced back to the source to actually deal with it.

Brain ruts...

Have you ever seen the huge tyre tracks that have been formed in a dirt road when a heavy truck has driven over it again and again, in its wet mud state? Once the mud dries out, it's nearly impossible for a smaller vehicle to move out of those tyre ruts - they will draw any vehicle into them, and keep it in that track, unless they are washed away in the rain and new ruts are formed. Or the vehicle needs to choose to take a completely different route. That's a good analogy for the way our thoughts work.

I'm not a neurological expert, but I have learned enough about the way the brain works through my own life experience. Speaking in layman's terms, our brain is like a computer that stores information in folders. Everything gets stored and filed - experiences good and bad - and emotions are attached to those experiences. The way we think about those experiences form pathways in our mind that are recorded as well. Every time we experience something, our brain rifles back into the folders of stored information, and looks for the correct filed emotional response to this situation we're encountering. Therefore, it is possible to think something long enough, that it causes a brain- rut and our brain's response to that situation will always take us down that path -

regardless of whether it is true or not. Our perception of a situation will be defined by whether or not we have thought the right thing in the first place.

That's scary… but it is also possible to change.

Feelings follow thoughts…

I heard a story recently, of a woman who was sick of her marriage and wanted a divorce. She had 'fallen out of love' with her husband, and didn't want to be with him anymore. Things had become so bad in their relationship that she actually believed she hated him and wanted to really hurt him. So, she made a decision that rather than leave him on a low note, the most devastatingly cruel thing she could do would be to act as if everything was fantastic, treat him really kindly and lovingly, and then, three months down the track, when he was completely unsuspecting, end the marriage with no warning! So, she set about treating him with respect, acting as if she loved him, training her mind to think great thoughts about him so her actions would appear genuine, and 'pretending' everything was great. After three months, when the time came to 'drop the bomb' on him, she realised she was no longer play-acting, but had actually fallen in love with her husband again. Even though her motive had been to deceive and hurt him, her disciplined, intentional thoughts, translating into actions, actually turned the course of her heart around, and their marriage was restored and flourished. Especially as the new thoughts were based on what was actually the original truth.

Here's the thing: thoughts are really like these nebulous things that float around in our head. We can't choose a thought or control its emerging, but we can choose whether or not we allow it to settle and take up residence. I get annoyed when a salesman knocks on my door, trying to sell the latest electricity/energy contract, mostly because they tend to come around dinner time. And because, if I let him in, he can be jolly persuasive. I can't control the fact that the salesman has come to my door, but I can decide whether I will open the door or not. If I do, however, foolishly choose to open the door, it's not too late. I can still politely say, *"No thank you, I'm not interested,"* and SHUT THE DOOR! When we have a thought that is akin to that pesky salesman, we always have a choice. We can recognise the pesky salesman for who he is, and not open the door to him. In other words, we don't even let that thought alight - we know it's wrong, so we shrug it off immediately. Sometimes, however, we do make the mistake of opening the door to the salesman, even though we know we don't really want what he's offering. When we have allowed ourselves to open the door to a wrong thought, we have to then discipline ourselves to look at that thought, and make the decision to close the door on it from then. *Barricade the road that goes Nowhere...* This is a process that takes time and effort. But it's worth it.

EVERY thought...

This process is true of good and bad thoughts alike. The Bible says in 2 Corinthians 10:5:

"We demolish arguments and every pretension that sets itself up against the knowledge of God, and we take captive every thought to make it obedient to Christ." (NIV)

Some thoughts may be reasonably neutral in and of themselves, but dwelling on them may eventually lead us to an unhealthy emotional place. So we take captive EVERY thought, hold it up to the light of God and His Word, and, if it's one that fits with God's heart and character, and lines up with the truth of Scripture, it can stay. If it's not a thought that is in harmony with Scripture and the character of a God-follower, then quickly deal with it. Barricade that road to nowhere. As you become more disciplined in this process, it becomes easier, new brain-ruts start to form, and you start to walk in the freedom of the truth of Romans 12:2 *"... be transformed by the renewing of your mind!"* (NIV)

There's also a very good reason that Philippians 4:8 says:

"And now, dear brothers and sisters, one final thing. FIX your thoughts on what is TRUE, and honourable, and right, and pure, and lovely, and admirable. Think about things that are excellent and worthy of praise." (NLT)

Our feelings always follow our thoughts. Always. If we dwell on something long enough, we will begin to feel that thing, good or bad. So, *"FIX your thoughts... "* yet again, this is an action verb. Keenly and intentionally fill your mind with good thoughts, and your emotions will follow.

Catch them if you can...

Emotions are merely reflectors of truth, not necessarily truths themselves, as I have experienced many times in my life. They will reflect what I tell them to reflect, by way of my thoughts. They are very useful to give some framework to experiences, and, therefore, good servants, but we were never meant to be LED by our emotions, especially when they are prone to running rampant, tossed and whipped up by every wrong thought.

Proverbs 14:30 says:

"A sound mind makes for a robust body, but **runaway emotions** corrode the bones." (MSG)

You see, as I mentioned earlier, it is possible for me to wake up in a great mood, and yet, an hour later, be down in the dumps in my emotions, because of something wrong I've thought. Something even as ridiculous as, *"Oh no, I've got to tackle all that housework today!"* It would be much better for me to think, *"Right, housework today... awesome! I'm going to feel great when it's all done!"* It's a subtle change - it's not denying that the housework has to be done - but I'm choosing to tell my mind what to think about the task, and therefore my emotions will follow.

And come on you girls reading this book, surely you remember how easy it was to develop 'feelings' for some pimply teenage boy, simply because you heard a rumour that he had a crush on you. And the more you **thought** about it, the more you realised that, even though you had never noticed him before now, you suddenly had feelings for him too. Real emotions based on truth? Nope... just a reflection of something you've allowed yourself to think. The amazing fact is, as we discipline our thoughts to a greater extent, and keep clear in our thinking, we are going to ultimately be a lot more discerning and receptive to the voice of God, and the things He's whispering to us.

Here's a great example. Just recently, a friend of mine told me of her journey with dating her fiancee. She was tired of thinking about guys, and the emotional need that was driving her to find a boyfriend, and she'd come to that great place in her mind and soul where she was just running hard in the purposes of God, and trusting Him for what He had for her in the future. In the midst of that freedom and clear thinking, God dropped a guy into her spirit, someone she was already in association with, but had never thought about in that way before, and, because it was God-directed, to her surprise, attraction followed almost instantly. They started dating, and, ten months later, they were engaged to be married and making plans to serve together in ministry. I'm not saying this is a formula and it always happens this way, but there is huge power in disciplining your thoughts and barricading that road that goes nowhere, especially in the teenage years. Save yourself a lot of heartbreak and wasted time, and keep your mind and heart clear, giving God the freedom He needs to speak to you, when the time is right.

Emotions affect your physical responses...

We had a visiting minister at church recently who is a trained clinical psychologist and counsellor, and I found it fascinating, as he talked about the power of our emotions and how they can even dictate a physical response in us. He shared an example of driving down the motorway and hearing a police siren behind him. Immediately, he looked at his speedometer, convinced he was speeding. As his mind carried him away, he started thinking about what he would say to the officer when he pulled him over, worse yet, what he would say to his WIFE when he had to show her the ticket... maybe he just shouldn't tell her about it at all.

As he thought more and more about this sticky situation he was in, he realised he was gripping the steering wheel, continually glancing back in the rear vision mirror, and it was at the exact moment that he noticed his palms were sticky with cold sweat, that the cop car sped by him. He had been chasing someone else! This guy had dwelt on something, his emotions had followed, and there was a physical response, yet it was not in any way based in truth. It was perceived truth - the cop was chasing someone, but it wasn't him!

Perception is not always truth...

A more poignant example is one, again, based in this whole journey with my image. I was so used to thinking, *"I am fat, and therefore a worthless human being,"* that it had ceased to become a conscious thought that I was able to grab and discard, but a stronghold in my mind. So much so that I wasn't even aware that my emotions were a direct result of that wrong thought process. And they would MESS ME UP. I could be feeling totally fine, at home by myself, confident and happy, but my emotional state would change dramatically and instantly, when I suddenly found myself in an environment where there were girls whom I perceived to be slim and beautiful. I didn't have to consciously think, *"Compared to these girls, I am fat and therefore a worthless human being,"* I just instantly felt it. And, because I had thought that way for so long, my brain would simply travel back along its rut, and rifle through the folders of my mind, to find the correct response to this situation. And then it would take me down the road of thinking that I was unlovable and not worth anything. Worse yet, while I was in that state, every interaction I would have with people would be marred and tainted by this powerful emotion. I would project these emotions onto Wayne especially, accusing him of not loving or accepting me. Was it true? No, not even vaguely. How shallow and foolish to base my worth as a human being, on a lie. I needed the freedom of the truth.

Now, I need to clarify here that what I'm talking about are the runaway, uncontrolled emotions that are the result of undisciplined thought patterns. There are times in life where our emotions do need to be respected, for example, in times of grief. Grief is the natural emotion that springs from a very real circumstance, and it does need to be honoured in order to process the loss of a loved one healthily. When my Dad passed away in 2010, I walked the natural path of grief, and that was emotionally debilitating for the first little while. But, after a period of time of healthily grieving, and allowing myself to feel what I needed to, there was no longer the sting of grief attached to my thoughts of him. Just lovely and treasured memories, even though my heart still missed him terribly. But there is also a time when the natural grief process may be completed, but we allow ourselves to stay in a place of emotional grief, where a spirit of grief can actually afflict us. I believe this, then, needs to be addressed and disciplined.

Simple doesn't mean easy...

There is absolute freedom waiting for us as we learn to discipline our thoughts, which will, in turn, affect how we feel. Whenever I have preached a message like this, I can see the light switch on in people's understanding as they say to me, *"Surely it can't be that simple?"* My response is always, *"Yes, it actually is that simple... but it's not necessarily easy."* It does take discipline and effort, something that we, in this quick-fix, 'I-want-it-now' society, are not necessarily accustomed to. The thought processes can be so ingrained that the emotions take a little while to get into line. The bottom line is, in the midst of the process, even if you don't feel like doing what's right, live by principle and do what you KNOW is right anyway. Everything within you may want to behave in a way that you know is not going to be good for you, but choose to live by what you know the Word of God says. It will be best for you in the long run. And have someone you can be accountable to, who can encourage you and pray for you along the journey.

Thoughts... feelings... words!

The natural recourse of undisciplined thoughts, creating undisciplined emotions, will almost always be an undisciplined tongue. I have so often found that, when I have been thinking the wrong thing, my emotions follow, and it's not too long before my speech backs that up. The words we speak are so very powerful and creative. It makes sense that, if we are created in the image of God - His DNA running through us - and He created everything with His spoken Word, we have the ability to do the same. The Bible says, that *"The power of life and death are in the tongue."* Funnily enough, the Bible doesn't add to that verse, *"... but only if you REALLY believe what you are saying!"* Your words, once spoken, are no respecter of your intentions or beliefs. Which is why it's so dangerous to speak out a negative word, especially against someone else, and then say, *"But I was only joking!"* Our tongue holds the power of life or death... full stop. And when we speak, whether we feel like we believe what we are saying or not, that word goes out to create the atmosphere around us.

Speech centre rules...

In his book, 'The Fourth Dimension'2, Dr Yonggi Cho talks about the neurological discovery that the speech centre in the brain, has dominion over all the body's nervous system. It's like the nervous system HAS to respond to instructions from command central.

Have a read of this:

"Then the neurosurgeon began to expand on their findings. He said that the speech nerve centre has such power over all the body that simply speaking can give one control over his body to manipulate it in the way he wishes. He said, "If someone keeps on saying, 'I'm going to become weak,' then right away, all the nerves receive that message and they say, 'Oh, let's prepare to become weak, for we have received instructions from our central communication that we should become weak.' They then, in natural sequence, adjust their physical attitude to weakness... Exactly as the Bible said 2000 years ago, it is so today. Medical science has just recently discovered this principle. This one neurosurgeon said that people should keep saying to themselves, 'I am young, I am able, I can do the work of a young person, no matter what my chronological age is.' The nerves of that person will become alive and receive power and strength from the nerve centre."

Proverbs 18:21 says:

"Words kill, words give life; they're either poison or fruit - YOU CHOOSE!" (MSG)

What an incredibly powerful twelve words! You choose what you want to fill your atmosphere with, both in your own life and the life of those you interact with!

Prophesy to the atmosphere...

Let's take this back to the analogy of the housework. I might wake up in the morning feeling fine, and then a thought occurs, *"Oh no, I've got to tackle all that housework today!"* Instantly, I start to feel all the effects of that undisciplined thought, and, as I get up out of bed, dragging my feet, with a weighty sigh, I exclaim, *"I just can't be bothered!"* And the atmosphere I have created is one of lethargy and laziness, as I drag myself through the task accordingly. Or worse, I don't do the housework at all.

I know this seems like a lightweight sort of example, but sometimes they are the best because we recognise ourselves in them! We've all spoken those sorts of words, haven't we? We've all willingly put a paintbrush, colour pallet and canvas in the hands of an undisciplined emotion, and it's painted exactly the picture IT desires to! Whenever we utter, *"I don't know what's wrong with me, I just feel..."* and then we follow it up with some negative statement, we are creating that atmosphere around us.

The opposite spirit is key...

My advice? Shut your trap, and speak out something in the opposite spirit, **especially** when you don't feel like it. Even if your thoughts are running wild, and your emotions are following in hot pursuit, you still have the power and ability to choose your words and stop that train in its tracks, before it reaches the point of no return. There have been so many times when I have had to choose to 'speak to my soul', and encourage myself with straight Scripture, when I'm feeling the opposite. I may be walking through a situation, my thoughts are running rampant, and I'm feeling like all is hopeless. But then I read something in the Word, and as I physically speak out the goodness and faithfulness of God, declaring His love and sovereignty, the atmosphere around me starts to change, and so do my emotions. Freedom! King David learnt the power of this soul-speech, and how to buoy himself up in God. He was the one who wrote, in Psalm 42:

"When my soul is in the dumps, I rehearse everything I know of You... Fix my eyes on God - soon I'll be praising again. He puts a smile on my face. He's my God!" (MSG)

When I was in the thick of the physical image journey, I didn't understand this principle about the power of the words I spoke and the freedom, or in my case death, associated with them. I would constantly voice my emotions when I was in a bad way, and the atmosphere around me was heavy and tiresome, especially for Wayne who felt the constant pressure to reassure me. But now, when I'm tempted to speak out negative words about my image, or anything else for that matter, I feel the heavy weight of death associated with those words. I feel that weight almost tangibly, and those words become repugnant to me, because I know what the atmosphere will feel like once they have escaped my lips. So I try my best to guard my tongue and refuse to speak out what my emotions are longing to voice. It's just too dangerous, and it creates death. I want my soul to live in freedom.

Written in black and white...

You recognise the difference in an atmosphere where there have been life-words spoken out, rather than critical, judgemental words of death, don't you? And the opposite is true; you can feel the effects in your own soul when you've just had a good old moan session to someone, about another person or situation. Rather than give you the desired, *"I just need to offload,"* release, it binds you up in your soul. So here are a good few scriptures to back up this 'little' truth about the power of the tongue!

"For everything we know about God's Word is summed up in a single sentence: Love others as you love yourself. That's an act of true freedom. If you bite and ravage each other, watch out - in no time at all you will be annihilating each other, and where will your precious freedom be then?" (Galations 5:15 MSG)

"That's a life shaped by things and feelings instead of by God... But you know better now, so make sure it's all gone for good: bad temper, irritability, meanness, profanity, dirty talk." (Colossians 3:5-8 MSG)

"No retaliation. No sharp-tongued sarcasm. Instead, bless - that's your job, to bless. You'll be a blessing and also get a blessing." (1 Peter 3:8 MSG)

And finally, the absolute clincher...

"It only takes a spark, remember, to set off a forest fire. A careless or wrongly placed word out of your mouth can do that. By our speech we can ruin the world, turn harmony into chaos, throw mud on a reputation, send the whole world up in smoke and go up in smoke with it, smoke right from the pit of hell!... With our tongues we bless God our Father; with the same tongues we curse the very men and women He made in His image. Curses and blessings out of the same mouth! My friends this can't go on." (James 3:5-10 MSG)

I love The Message translation... so eloquent. So very... CONVICTING! But it's there in God's Word, in black and white. Watch the words you speak, both over yourself and over others. And I'm not just talking about negative words, but even words whose original meaning is completely different from the way it is now being used: *"Haha fail! Shame!"* is used as a comical putdown when someone does something embarrassing, but I'm not entirely sure why speaking failure and shame over someone else's life is funny? *"Sick!"* is no longer a word used to describe a physical ailment. *"Mean"* is now a good thing, and who decided that

"Wicked!" was actually awesome? I'd kind of like to return to the time when *"gay"* was just a happy emotion!

Power of a name...

I'm jesting, but I will tell you a story of a beautiful friend of mine, Adrian Lindsey, who learnt the power of what seemed like an innocent word - her name - in a very real and life changing way.

Adrian is African-American and, from a young age, rather than going by her full name, was known to others as Dree. She would introduce herself, and insist others referred to her as Dree. For many years, Adrian felt tired and weary as she struggled with low self-esteem, and depressive and oppressive thoughts and feelings. It was if there was always a thick cloud of low emotion over her. She is a Christian and fully knows Christ as her Saviour and Redeemer, yet still she battled with this depressive thing despite being prayed for countless times.

Then, a few years ago, Adrian learnt what her name actually meant. Adrian, means 'dark and lovely' (which she very much is!), and 'wealthy or rich', but Dree means 'tedious, dreary, to suffer and endure'. After learning this information, and some prayer with her husband to break through this shield of weariness, depression and low self-esteem, Adrian made a physical, life altering decision, and asked people to no longer call her Dree, but return to calling her Adrian. With the prayer and the name change she was almost instantly set free, and her life emotionally turned around. You see, every time she had previously introduced herself as Dree, what she was basically declaring was, *"Hello, I'm weary, dreary and tedious,"* and every time someone called her name, they were declaring the same thing to her, and over her life! No wonder she struggled for so long to get out from under such a stronghold - those words had literally created the atmosphere of her world around her.

Our enemy is after our praise...

Yes, there is huge power in the negative words we speak or that are spoken over us. But there is also huge impact when we NEGLECT to speak positive words into the atmosphere. Let me explain.

The enemy has always been after our praise. Firstly, because he HATES to hear God being praised. His aim was to be worshipped like God, and that was the very reason he was cast down from heaven. You have to understand, Lucifer held a privileged position in heaven - an archangel, beautiful to a fault, and extremely gifted musically. You could say his main job was to lead the angels in heaven, in worship. Somewhere along the way, he desired the praise that only God was worthy of, and, from the day he was cast out of heaven, he's been chasing that praise ever since.

Secondly, I do believe he understands the power that is in the tongue to bless and to curse. When he presented himself before God, along with all the angels, and was given permission to mess with Job, he wasn't really concerned about whether or not Job had a mental breakdown from the enormous emotional pressure he was under. He wasn't waiting around to see whether Job would cave and bawl like a baby. He didn't even care if Job spat the dummy and let a bunch of negative toxic words flow, although I'm sure he does revel in the darkness of our speech at times. He didn't actually care at all what happened to Job physically or emotionally in the end. All he wanted was to hear Job curse God. He wanted to influence Job's language...

Too often we think the enemy is out to 'get' us. We talk about being under spiritual attack when things go wrong, and we put far too much emphasis on the devil. He revels in our blame, because he's getting the glory, which is what he's always been after! But if we could simply choose to use those circumstances as an opportunity to praise - to put positive words into the atmosphere - he's lost!

While touring with the Parachute Band, we were ministering at Saddleback Church in Orange County, California, the same weekend that Pastor Kay Warren was highlighting an AIDS awareness campaign. There was a guest in the service that day - an African Princess, who, in her late twenties, had not only nursed both her parents suffering from Aids, and watched them die, but was also HIV positive herself. She was an incredible Christian young woman, a sense of absolute royalty and humility about her, and God had given her a platform to speak as an AIDS advocate worldwide. And when she shared her testimony, I was completely humbled and challenged, especially when she uttered this statement: *"I count it an honour that God would see me worthy to carry this disease for His glory!"*

I'm pretty sure I had been complaining about a common cold and how miserable I felt, not too long prior to this encounter…

Be intentional for goodness sake!

What power there is in **consciously** and **intentionally** filling the atmosphere around our life with PRAISE, especially when it's the exact opposite of what we feel like doing. If the enemy can silence our praise, he will do it. In fact, he will do whatever he can to stop God receiving the praise He is due. And I'm not just talking about physical praise words spoken or sung in church on Sunday. Because the fact is, it's possible to sing the right 'praise' words in church on Sunday, but it becomes merely lip-service if, for the rest of the week, we moan about how terrible our life is, how bad we're feeling, and how nothing is going right. We backbite, gossip and dishonour others. And, as we speak words of negativity over our situations, ourselves and others, the enemy has ever so subtly achieved his goal. The tongue that was meant to be used for praise, has been redeemed by another master altogether, and that's all the enemy has to do. In effect, he has actually stolen God's praise as we have chosen to speak negativity into the atmosphere. And we don't even realise that one affects the other…

Because praise doesn't just encompass those specific words...

Every time you say, *"My life sucks!"* the enemy is silencing your praise.
Every time you say, *"I HATE the way he/she does..."* the enemy is silencing your praise.
Every time you say, *"I just can't be bothered trying, nothing's going to change anyway..."* the enemy is silencing your praise.
Every time you say, *"I feel..."* and follow it up with something negative, the enemy is silencing your praise.

Yes, with every undisciplined, negative word you speak, the enemy is silencing your praise, and robbing you of the chance to honour and praise God in the midst of the circumstances, thereby giving Him glory...

Written words are just as powerful...

I feel it important to mention here that I'm not just talking about audible words, but written words also. In this technological, information-saturated age we are living in, tweets and Facebook status updates and comments, are just as powerful as spoken words, in fact often more so. Because the immediate audience is so much larger. I've often said that writing a Facebook status, or commenting on someone's wall, is like having a private conversation, with 1000 people listening in! Use social media wisely, and choose your words carefully - just because they are written doesn't mean you are not responsible for them, and just because you think no-one hears them, they are just as loud - both positive and negative.

Praise breaks chains...

Yes, what power there is in filling the atmosphere around our life with praise... especially when we **don't feel** like it. In the book of Acts, we read the account of Paul and Silas, being thrown into prison yet again, for preaching and holding fast to the truth of Jesus as Messiah. If anyone had reason to maybe feel a little sorry for themselves, it would be these two. They had been beaten, shipwrecked, falsely accused, and gone hungry. Paul himself had been stoned and received 39 lashes five times, had been adrift at sea, and threatened by all manner of human and natural terrors. Imagine if Paul and Silas, locked in prison, after being beaten and left naked, had given into their thoughts and emotions, and voiced them. But they chose praise, based on their recognition of the goodness of God. And the result was their physical freedom, and the spiritual freedom and salvation of a whole region. The jailer, who saw them miraculously released, got saved and went on to be the 'pastor' of the church in that area of Ephesus. As they released praise into the atmosphere, chains fell off, and salvation visited the prison. So much freedom and breakthrough, for themselves and others, rode on their praise… imagine if they hadn't.

Imagine what may be riding on your choice to praise today… or not to!

"I can't tell you how much I long for you to enter this wide open, spacious life. We didn't fence you in. The smallness you feel comes from within you. Your lives aren't small but you're living them in a small way. I'm speaking as plainly as I can and with great affection. Open up your lives. Live openly and expansively!" (2 Corinthians 6:11-13 MSG)

The free life is spacious…

I am so thankful for freedom. Freedom is like a cold, refreshing drink on a hot, dry, dusty day. It truly satisfies. I am thankful for the boundaries and restraints that I have placed around certain areas in my life, because of my love for Jesus, and because I want to stay free in my soul. The free life in the Spirit of God is spacious, roomy, open, and light. The possibilities are endless when you're living in that space!

Even though I am still a work in progress and not yet fully arrived, I can honestly tell you, this journey to disciplining my thoughts, emotions and words, has been the largest factor in attaining freedom in every area in my life so far. Remember what the Bible (Libby paraphrase!) says: *"You will be transformed, as you renew your mind, take captive every thought, don't live a life shaped by things and feelings, and remember you hold the power of life and death in your tongue."* I encourage you, no I DARE you, to put this into practise and you will start to walk in increased freedom.

Earned freedom gains authority...

Any area we have gained freedom in, we then also have authority for. If we can truly start to see the freedom we have, especially in the way we use our tongue, we have authority then in that area to speak words prophetically into the atmosphere as well. Just like our Creator Father, our words, when in line with His will and Word, have the ability to go out into the future and create a different reality! You will read in chapter 9, that my vocal cord journey was a prime example of this. In the midst of physical damage, I needed to hear what God's reality was, and, even though it was in contradiction to the physical circumstances, I believe as I spoke out the Word of God, my words, in unity with His revealed rhema Word to me, went out and created a new reality.

And we don't need to be on a platform preaching to a church of thousands, to bring the voice and heart of God to someone else. Our everyday conversations can become saturated and full with the very prophetic weight of God's voice, when we allow ourselves to hear His heart and just confidently and naturally communicate that. Give it a try!

The bubble burst?

When our children were very young, I would always say to them, *"Do you know, you are **THE** most beautiful children in the whole* *world?"* And Gracie's response was always, *"I know we are Mummy!"* One night, we were going to pick Wayne up from the airport, and we went to McDonald's as a treat first. As was my habit, while we were eating, I said to them again, *"Do you know you are **THE** most beautiful children in the whole world?"* but this night, six year old Gracie said, *"Mummy, **EVERY** parent says that about their own children!"* I felt a little sad, realising that she was finally onto me, and the bubble of perception had finally been burst. But in the next breath, Gracie matter-of-factly and confidently stated, *"But those kids aren't Mummy… cause **WE** are!"* She still fully believed that what I told her was the truth! I know this is just a fun little anecdote, but as I mentioned earlier, our perception of something will shape our reality, whether it's true or not. And therefore, it is so vitally important to renew our thinking as the foundation, based ONLY on the Word of God, and what He says about us.

In chapter 37 of the book of Ezekiel, Ezekiel was shown a valley of dry bones, bones that had been the army of Israel, but were now dried up with no life and no hope. God first showed Ezekiel the bones as they were - a picture of the current reality - but then told him to speak to the bones, telling them of their new reality. Ezekiel watched as the bones rattled together and began to re-form into bodies with flesh, muscle, sinew and skin. God then told Ezekiel to prophesy the breath of life to return to them, and, as he spoke the words, breath returned and they were alive, ready to move! Now this is interesting, because, even though the bones were now standing, alive and ready for action, and God had told Ezekiel who they were - the whole house of Israel - God still told Ezekiel to LISTEN to what the bones themselves were saying: *"Our bones are dried up, our hope is gone, there's nothing left of us."* (Ezekiel 37:11 MSG) Once Ezekiel had heard the bones' negative confession, even in the face of a changed reality, God told Ezekiel to prophesy again, this time telling them GOD'S view of them!

There may be a situation that you are praying about for someone else, you may be 'standing in the gap' for them in a desperately hopeless situation, devoid of life, and they have lost hope. But you just may hold the key to seeing their destiny change, if you will hear the Word of God for them, and continue to send it out into the atmosphere. Your words hold prophetic weight, when they line up with what God is saying. Prophesy into the atmosphere of your own life and your words will change your world!

Chapter Seven
Expensive Worship

I read a book a number of years ago, called 'Enter the Worship Circle', by Ben Pasley, and, to me, it is still one of the most challenging and fresh insights into worship I have read. One of many significant quotes from this book is this:

"We all want to be in the presence of greatness, and we all want a chance to react to awe-inspiring things... to personally respond to greatness... The object of our worship will prove our hearts. It proves what's inside of us by the very notion that we would give it honour... As we look for something to receive our greatest affection we must make sure that it is truly worthy. If it does not engage our sense of wonder for eternity, then it is an inferior, temporary object that will impart to us an inferior, temporary sense of being. What we worship has everything to do with how we live, what we love, and what we will become in this life and the life beyond."[1]

Something great happens in us as we personally respond to greatness! I watched the opening ceremony of the 2012 Olympics while we were away on a ministry trip in Brisbane, Australia, and I had tears running down my face as the New Zealand team entered the arena. It was possibly a touch of patriotism, but mostly because I recognised these were men and women of incredible talent who had disciplined themselves, honed their craft, and worked so very hard to have the privilege of bearing their country's name. And even though I am not an athlete (I can sense the look of shock on your face!), I love watching the Olympics - track, swimming and high-diving are among my favourites - because there is something glorious about these athletes' greatness and disciplined ability! I know I could never compete with that ability, but also wouldn't want to because then it wouldn't be as glorious! There's something so freeing about acknowledging gifting, ability and power, so infinitely greater than my own. My spirit responds accordingly, and I somehow feel richer for the experience... it's almost akin to worship!

Bishop Joseph Garlington put it like this:

"Worship, is to act as an inferior before a superior."[2]

It's almost like the right and natural order of things comes into line. As we lift up Jesus, He lifts us up. As we see who He is, He shows us who we are! Which is where the truth of Romans 12:1-2 really comes into play:

"Therefore, I urge you, brothers and sisters, in view of God's mercy, to offer your bodies as a living sacrifice... this is your true and proper worship." (NIV)

In other words, in light of all He has done, in view of His greatness, give Him your life as worship. Personally respond to His greatness.

I'm not an idol-worshipper!

Again, as with everything in life, this understanding of worship is a journey, yet we are inherently wired for it. Christians and non-Christians alike, all worship something, and often many 'gods' at once! But God is always bringing us back to that place of sacrifice and surrender, not because He wants us to be under the thumb like whimpering subjects, but because He wants us to experience the freedom of intimacy with Him, that we were created for. And, in order for that to happen, the other 'gods' have got to bow!

You might ask: *"What other gods? I don't follow another religion. I'm a Christian! I go to church on Sunday - usually twice! I'm EVEN on the worship team!"*

But the real question is, how does being a Christian and being on the worship team, affect and influence your *"everyday, ordinary life - your sleeping, eating, going-to-work, and walking-around life"?* (Romans 12:2 MSG). How often do we very easily, and often conveniently, box worship in as something we just do at church on a Sunday, and something we practise at Wednesday night rehearsal?

Seriously?

Living worship?

Well, you must realise I'm not just talking about music and singing songs here, right? I guess I was fortunate, in a strange way, to have grown up in a church where the 'worship' didn't really grab my heart, so I wasn't emotionally carried away by it. It was just stand up, sing a hymn and sit down again. Wayne grew up in a church where the whole service was referred to as worship, which was a little closer to the truth. But then I started hearing about your life being lived out as worship, and this was a little harder to figure out.
How do I live worship?
How do I become a living sacrifice? That sounds messy...
If all I've known to bring is a song, but this isn't really the essence of worship, then what is, and how do I do it?

And it comes back to this Ben Pasley quote:

"The object of our worship will prove our hearts. It proves what's inside of us by the very notion that we would give it honour... What we worship has everything to do with how we live, what we love and what we will become in this life and the life beyond."
Worship has EVERYTHING to do with how we live...
Worship has EVERYTHING to do with what we love...
Worship has EVERYTHING to do with what we will become...

So, it is possible for me to sing a song, in the atmosphere of worship on Sunday, and fully mean it then, but contradict that song on Monday, in the way I conduct myself in my workplace...

It is possible for me to profess my devoted and undivided love for God, in the atmosphere of worship on Sunday, and fully mean it then, but fill my week up with work, T.V, sport, others and 'me'-time, leaving Him the dregs of a tired, bedtime, bless-me prayer...

It is possible for me to declare that my life will honour Him, in the atmosphere of worship on Sunday, and fully mean it then, but negate that declaration by not treating other people in a way that is honourable to them, or to God...

It is possible for me to confess that He is all I need, in the atmosphere of worship on Sunday, and fully mean it then, but spend the rest of the week striving and grasping at people and things, to meet my needs...

Somewhere along the journey, worship has to start costing us more than a song... it needs to shape the way we live, it needs to shape the way we love, and it needs to cost us our life... full stop!

Time for a story...

For something to be worth something, we need to know its value. This is not always measured in monetary terms, but something we value will always have had some sort of cost associated with it and, therefore, it will be worth something to us. When I first moved away from home, my Mum gave me a whole lot of my English grandmother's china to take with me. Tea cups and side plates, to just use everyday. So I did! I enjoyed drinking coffee in these cups - they were the right density, not too thick or thin - just perfect. They were just my everyday crockery. The year after Wayne and I were married, however, we were walking past an antique shop, one day, and saw some pieces of this same china in the window... and they were valuable! One dinner plate was worth $55 (this is over 20 years ago too) and the teapot, $300. Wayne's immediate reaction was: *"Let's hock it off!"* However, my eyes were suddenly opened to the true value of this china - there was great worth now associated with it - so I packed it up in a box and didn't use it again for many years!

How sad is that? And yet there have been times in history where men, understanding the worth and value of the Word of God, have then made it so sacred, holy and inaccessible, that common men were not allowed to read His Word for themselves, or utter His Name, and religious bondage followed. God always intended worship and His Word, to be for the individual, worked out in the everyday-ness of life, because His heart for us is RELATIONSHIP! Just like my grandmother's china, which has reappeared in my cupboard, and been used for many 'tea-parties' by my daughter!

So how do I make my worship costly - not inaccessible and sacred - yet still expensive to me?

Confetti, can-opener worship...

When Wayne and I were touring in the Parachute Band, we would tour for three weeks at a time, totaling about four months a year, and our kids, who were much younger at the time, did not tour with us, but stayed home with Nanny Abbey. Invariably, we would leave for the first tour of the year in February, and usually before Wayne's birthday, so Gracie and Josh didn't often get to celebrate with their Daddy. One year, when Gracie was about eight years old and Josh was five, we were to leave a little later for a tour and so got to have Wayne's birthday together at home, so we decided we would eat out at a restaurant and celebrate all together. A few days prior, Gracie told me she wanted to buy her Daddy a gift, and asked if I could take her shopping to buy something with her own money. I put aside what I was doing, and off we trooped to the $2 Shop, where Gracie bought Wayne... wait for it... a can opener! A CAN OPENER! In my mind, a block of chocolate would have been more appropriate, and it would have been more convenient for me just to pick up a block, along with the other groceries, when I went to the supermarket. But this was not about appropriateness or convenience, this was about a little girl buying her Daddy a gift, with her own money, from her own heart.

We came home, and I watched as Gracie began to create homemade wrapping paper to wrap the gift. That thing was covered in love hearts, and flowers, and stickers - colourful to a fault - a glorious, eight-year-old's, artistic mess! And then, THE CARD! White paper folded over and decorated, again with flowers, and hearts, and stickers, and then filled with words of love for her Daddy, (Gracie was a fantastically phonetic speller at that age, so I'm not sure if the message was entirely clear!)

But then the 'piece de resistance' (that's French guys!) I watched, as over the next few days, Gracie and Josh took turns with a hole-punch, punching hundreds upon hundreds of holes in pieces of paper, and collecting the little white paper dots in a plastic bag. Their plan was to throw confetti all over Wayne as he walked out the front door of our house, to head to the restaurant on the big night! A huge birthday fanfare! A costly endeavour - in both time and heart!

The night came, and Gracie and Josh waited to the side of our front door for Wayne to exit. Unfortunately, they were standing down-wind, and, as Wayne came through the door and they threw the handfuls of confetti, pretty much all of it blew back on themselves and the garden, missing Wayne completely! I can remember him looking bemused and slightly confused at what had ALMOST happened, but, because he is an awesome Dad, he appreciated the effort (once explained to him!)

We arrived at the restaurant, our food was ordered and delivered, and we enjoyed the time together. And then came the precious, most important moment - the 'Giving of the Gift'. I have to admit, I was a little nervous. Would Wayne appreciate the effort that had gone into that homemade wrapping paper? Would he revel in the words of love scrawled painstakingly in the homemade card? Would he even LIKE the can opener?

My fears were allayed as I became spectator of one of the most simple, yet precious exchanges between father and daughter. The look of delight on Wayne's face as he took the gift in his hand and studied every aspect of the wrapping paper, was equal to Gracie's look of joy in watching her Daddy, knowing she was the initiator of that delight. My eyes started tearing up as he read the message in the card (some translation necessary!), words of adoration, appreciation and love from daughter to Daddy. The anticipation and eagerness on her face - the absolute joy at bringing her Daddy simple pleasure could not be bought with money! And then, the unwrapping of the gift, and, no, Wayne did not fail in his fatherly responsibilities, *"A CAN OPENER! Just what I always wanted!"* was his 'delighted' response, culminating in hugs, kisses and overflowing love. And the joy on Gracie's face could not be contained, or even physically captured on film!

Convenient and calculated or costly?

I tell you this story to illustrate a point, and the allegory is pretty clear and simple. This did actually happen, and, at the time, it painted the most beautiful picture of the worship exchange that takes place between father and child. And I don't mean an act of worship that is confined to within the walls of a church building on a Sunday morning, and packaged up in a song, but is the overflow of a life lived in RELATIONSHIP together!

As I mentioned, it would have been much easier for me to buy a block of Wayne's favourite chocolate at the supermarket, wrap it up myself, and just get Gracie to sign the bottom of a .99cent card with the stock standard birthday greeting. It would have still been a gift, there would have still been a card - everything would have LOOKED right. But Gracie wanted to give him something that she had chosen, that cost her her own money, time and effort. It wasn't beautifully wrapped with the corners all neatly tucked in, and the cellotape perfectly even, but it was a gift that was weighty with love and sacrifice.

You see, how often do we worship out of convenience to us? So much of our worship in church is exactly that - convenient. Singing a song that someone else has written, wrapped up in a perfect arrangement. And it can even have the right appearance. Carefully, calculated worship that costs us nothing really… a block of chocolate and a .99cent card written by someone else, that we simply sign our name at the bottom of. Even worse, we sign a hasty *"Love me,"* with an ambiguous, *"love me… love me… LOVE ME! Heal ME, touch ME, free ME, provide for ME!"* and our worship has become all about what we can get out of it, like making a withdrawal from the spiritual ATM machine, rather than delighting the heart of our Father… and it has COST US NOTHING!

What does your worship look like at the moment? Is it convenient and calculated worship, or is it can-opener, confetti worship? And you know I'm not just talking about what you do in church on Sunday.

My costly worship…

While touring in the Parachute Band, I would often have people say to me, *"Wow, it must be really hard doing what you guys do - gruelling travel, late nights, plane flights. God bless you for the huge sacrifice you make!"* While I truly appreciated their heartfelt sentiment - and please hear me on this because I could understand their perspective on it - I had to honestly say the actual physical touring was not as it may have seemed. We had the enormous privilege of visiting many different nations, leading worship in incredible churches and at festivals, and rubbing shoulders with some phenomenal leaders, pastors and musicians, all around the world. We got to stay in hotels, we were taken out to restaurants to eat, and we were really treated like royalty. Yes, there were late nights and early morning plane flights, but there was also the privilege and joy of seeing people respond in worship, and lives being changed! It was an incredible season in our lives.

But do you know where my worship became costly? Three days before we would leave for a tour, I would start to feel that familiar heart-lurch as I looked at my children - they were only five and two years old when we first started touring - and I knew I had to leave them for three weeks at a time and fly to the other side of the world. I would hug them a little more, I would spend longer tucking them in at night, I would sometimes just stand in their room and watch them as they slept, and my heart would feel sick at the thought of those three weeks ahead, even though I knew God had called us to this. I would carry their photos with me overseas, and show them off to anyone who would look, as it made me feel more connected to them! Joshie especially, being only two, was soft and squashy with a fuzzy little head, and it would not be unusual for me to ask a mother if I could just hug her little one if he so painfully reminded me of Josh. The feeling of standing in a hotel room on the other side of the world, and imagining what they would be doing at that very moment, made my heart physically hurt, and is still so familiar. I remember, once, leaving for the airport to fly to America, crying and feeling like the worst mother in the world, but having to trust my children's care into the hands of our nanny, while Gracie lay on the couch, almost delirious with a high fever and vomiting. And this was not an isolated case - in fact, more often than not, one of my children would be sick or needing me as we left for tour.

And this became my worship.

Leading people into God's presence was a privilege…
Leaving my children to do it, cost me…

What's the cost?

God is always looking for that thing that is most expensive to you. It may be laying down your desires and dreams. It may be making a decision based on what you believe God wants, not what you want - simple obedience becomes your worship. It may mean laying down a relationship, or a career, YOUR plans for YOUR future. Your dignity and reputation may be a costly sacrifice. It may mean changing your thought patterns, and the habits you comfortably and safely hide behind. Are you willing to lay down the things most precious to you, in order to gain a greater level of intimacy with Him?

C.S Lewis said:

"There are far, far better things ahead, than any we leave behind."[3]

Costly worship, rather than just singing songs, will always have a post-blessing effect in our lives. It's a spiritual law: *"What you sow, you will be sure to reap!"* When we worship God in a way that costs us, we are sowing seeds that will yield a harvest in the future. Obviously this should not be our motivation for worship, and knowing that the first and greatest result is this increased intimacy with our Father, does tend to cause any wrong motivation to turn sour in our mouths. There's something about knowing we have brought Him pleasure with our worship, just as Gracie brought her Daddy pleasure, not necessarily with the gift but the heart intent behind the gift, that is the greatest blessing of all!

Blessing on the other side...

King David was known as a man after God's own heart, so he knew what it was to have intimate relationship with his God, yet, there were still very obvious areas in his life that needed to be surrendered and laid down as worship to Him. His security being one! Possibly, because he was wanting to feel secure in the knowledge of the strength of his army - false security built on man rather than on God's strength alone - David sinned by taking a census of his people when he had been expressly told not to. There was a consequence to pay, and he was given three choices. After choosing the consequence with the least ramifications for the nation, David knew he then needed to make restitution for his own sin personally. He needed to get his heart right with his God again. Broken and grief-stricken, he passed by the threshing floor of Araunah, the Jebusite, and he decided he would build an altar there and sacrifice to God. So he asked the Jebusite if he could purchase his field. The Jebusite, recognising his King, graciously offered to give him the field and all the provisions necessary to make his sacrifice. David's response was: *"No, for I refuse to offer sacrifices to my God that have cost me NOTHING!"* He understood the power of costly worship. Even in the midst of his guilt, shame and pain, David knew He needed to worship God with an expensive sacrifice, because the cost of that was nowhere near as great as the cost of an unrestored relationship with Him. The beautiful thing about this account is that the threshing floor, where David sacrificed, in the midst of his brokenness and guilt, became the foundation of King Solomon's Temple - the most glorious temple of worship ever known to man. You have no idea what your costly worship is creating in your future, both for you and for generations to come.

I do believe God counts our costly worship precious, and holds it close. There is an exchange that takes place because of what we have been willing to lay down, in order to have greater intimacy with Him. He does not take it lightly. In the midst of those touring years, there were many times I would cry out to God, *"You've got to hold my children."* I needed to know that the costly worship I had given Him was safe and of value to Him. There were times when I would wonder if Gracie and Josh would even catch the whole worship deal, because we were away so often and, at one time, they were regularly attending three different churches - ours, when we were home, the church where our nanny was children's pastor, plus another she sometimes attended in the evenings as her church didn't hold an evening service. My biggest fear was that they would grow up to resent God for taking their parents away from them. But we made a point of never apologising to them for being in ministry, always including them with tour updates, and answered prayers when we were away. This is a point of encouragement to you parents who are in ministry - instil in your kids a love for what you do and, more importantly, a love for the House of God, and take them on the journey with you, even if it's just reminding them how much a part of the bigger picture they are alongside you.

There was one especially poignant memory in our touring years, when we were possibly going to have to do a second tour to America right off the back of another, with only a three day turn around at home. I was feeling that familiar anguished mother's-heart emotion, and we were conflicted as to whether we could responsibly leave the kids again, or not. On advice of our nanny, I sat Gracie down, who was about nine at the time, and asked her what she felt about it. She had her back turned to me and I could make out tears rolling down her cheeks, as she said to me, *"Mummy, you have to go."* My heart was torn and I said to her, *"Baby, don't tell me what you THINK I want to hear. I want to know what you really feel about this - we're in this together as a family."* And as she turned around to face me, with tear stained cheeks, she replied, *"Mummy, if you and Daddy don't go, Joshie and I will be happy, but thousands of other people won't get to hear about Jesus. You have to go."*

In response to their own personal sacrifice, our kids have grown up with a huge understanding of both worship and ministry, and are now both, as a teenager and young adult, actively serving in worship at our church, and have been involved in evangelistic touring teams around New Zealand at a much younger age than we ever were. But, more importantly, both have had real, personal and intimate encounters with their God! I am so thankful! I believe the grace and mercy of God has flowed to our children, in part because God held our costly worship precious...

Psalm 61:8 says:

"I'll be the poet who sings your Glory, and live what I sing every day." (MSG)

This verse has been one of those life defining ones for me. For those of you reading this, especially those involved in leading worship in your church, my biggest prayer is that you would be one whose LIFE sings His glory, and, whatever you do in church on Sunday, would simply be the overflow of that life lived out as worship - worship that is costly and extravagant!

"Loved before I ever knew You
Chosen, called, renewed
Now my life will sing Your Glory
Salvation sing your song over me
Oh Christ the King, my Friend, my Peace
I live to worship You
  And I'll run to the Saving Arms
  Of the One who has loved me completely
  And I'll trust in the saving grace
  Of Christ The King, my Friend, my Peace"
- 'Saving Arms'[4]

Chapter Eight
Created For One-ness

"Lost in You, I'm overwhelmed
Face down in awe, so overwhelmed
How beautiful, how beautiful You are
I'm living to ever know
Your grace and Your mercy in overflow
How beautiful, how beautiful You are
>I stand amazed at You
>Falling in love with You

That One so holy as You, would let me see Your beautiful face
I can't believe that I'm free just to stand here with You
And worship You
>I see You, I worship You in this holy place."
>>-'Overwhelmed'[1]

"So here's what I want you to do, God helping you: Take your everyday, ordinary life - your sleeping, eating, going-to-work, and walking-around life - and place it before God as an offering. Embracing what God does for you is the best thing you can do for Him. Don't become so adjusted to your culture that you fit into it without even thinking. Instead, fix your attention on God. You'll be changed from the inside out. Readily recognise what He wants from you and quickly respond to it." (Romans 12:1-2 MSG)

Love demanded is not love...

What does God actually want from us? Our service? Our gifts and talents? Our worship? Our time? Our lives? All of these things, and yet none of them, if they are not born out of, and based in, a two-way love-relationship. We can serve Him, we can offer Him our gifts, and our time. We can even worship Him, and our lives be actively sold-out for His cause, yet all these things can just be religious posturing, and actually bind us up, if our hearts are not surrendered and falling more in love with who He is. No-one wants love and affection that is demanded of them, and not freely and joyously given. God is not some egotistical, power hungry deity who demands worship from us - yes, He is holy, just and awe-inspiring, and, therefore, worthy of worship, but He is also tender, intimate and close, and wants RELATIONSHIP with you every day, not just your Sunday service 'worship'.

For many years, Wayne and I have preached the message: *"We were created for worship."* It was not until recently that we began to realise that, although there is truth in this statement, there is a greater truth: We were created for 'one-ness', sin messed that up, and worship is the vehicle to help us return to that state of one-ness, or full intimacy, with our Creator!

Into the wilderness...

When the Israelites had finally been released from Egypt, they thought they were heading for the Promised Land. You see, again, for them, the destination was their goal and aim. But God was wanting to take them into the wilderness, so they could re-establish relationship, and worship Him. He wanted to show them His glory. He wanted to reconnect with His people again, His prized and treasured possession. Yes, He wanted to take them to the Promised Land, but there was a journey to be travelled first. What point would the abundance of the Promised Land be, without the restoration of relationship? God's people had lost relationship with Him in captivity, and He was bringing them out, so they could experience the fullness of intimacy and covering again.

At the base of Mount Sinai, God asked them to consecrate themselves for three days because He was getting ready to show them His glory. Why did He ask them to consecrate themselves? He got them out of Egypt, and now He needed to get Egypt out of them! They needed to prepare to meet the Holy God - they needed to address the wrong thinking, the captivity mindset, the victim mentality, the desire for a different place, even though that place had kept them bound in captivity! How often we do the same - long for a place or situation, or relationship we were caught in, because we haven't yet experienced the true joy and freedom of the relationship we were created for. He needed them to prepare themselves for a new way of thinking, a new way of living as God's people, a new relationship! He wasn't getting ready to terrify them with His fire, might, and power, although His glory did physically appear that way. He wanted to reveal the truth of who He was to them, and have them, as a people, respond.

But they blew it…

They were scared, so they told Moses to go and meet with God by Himself and just relay to them what He wanted to tell them. They were more comfortable with keeping this terrifying God well at arm's length. They missed the invitation! And it wasn't long before they started worshipping another god of their own making. You see, they were created for a relationship of intimacy, but they preferred a religion that they perceived didn't demand so much of them. Religion will always thrive where there is no relationship! And it stinks - I HATE religion!

Sacrifice is good for us…

When God asks us to lay down our lives as a living sacrifice, it's not because He wants to steal our joy, deprive us of life, and keep us downtrodden and under the thumb. He's actually wanting to bring us into greater freedom. He knows it's GOOD for us! He's wanting to reveal more of who He is to us, and connect with us in greater intimacy. But we need to understand who He truly is, and understand His character and nature in its entirety. Yes, He is Love, He is close and caring, but He is also Almighty God, He is

Holy, He is truly AWESOME (and I don't mean the watered-down awesome that we use to describe a good meal, movie, or someone's wardrobe choice for the day!)

The Shorter Catechism states that:

"The chief end of man is to glorify God and enjoy Him forever."[2]

These are not two individual statements that stand alone, while at the same time complementing each other. We can't say our chief end ONLY is to glorify God - all of Creation does that by default. And if we seek only to glorify God, but miss enjoying Him, then we can easily fall into the trap of thinking that just serving Him is enough. He wants more than service from us! He wants love, enjoyment, and relationship with us. We, as mankind, have the privilege of enjoying God forever! Somewhere along the way, especially for those of us who use their specific gifts to serve Him, God needs to separate the gift from the person, as that can so easily lead us down the path of becoming human 'doings' rather than human 'beings'.

Restless hearts find rest in Him...

Augustine made a beautiful statement:

"Thou hast formed us for Thyself, and our hearts are restless till they find rest in Thee."[3]

I love that! In all my years as a Christian, and especially more recently as a pastor, I have seen and talked to so many people as they struggle to find that place of rest, reconciliation and satisfaction in their souls. I have watched people, even as Christians, try to fill that void, with meaningless and temporal things that satisfy for a moment, but never truly quench the thirst and hunger we were all created with. And my advice is always simple and the same - find Jesus and fall in love with Him! God is jealous over us, in the most righteous and beautiful way possible! He longs for us, and yearns for relationship with His creation, us His children. And finding that place of intimacy with Him is like drinking a long, cool drink of iced water on a hot summer's day! Sorry, but room temperature Coca-cola just doesn't cut it!

This discovery of intimacy has been a large part of my journey. I know some people struggle with the idea of having an intimate relationship with God, as if we are confusing God and the way we worship Him with a Mills and Boon novel, yet, I wonder if they have the wrong idea of what true intimacy really is? Intimacy, in an earthly sense, always seems to be equated with something sexual, but I believe true intimacy relates more to an absolute emotional one-ness. It's possible to have sex without intimacy, and how empty that is, but the emotional one-ness that comes with an intimate marriage relationship just makes the physical act so much better. And this marriage relationship - emotional one-ness - is the closest picture of what an intimate relationship with our Father looks like. Remember, Jesus is coming back for His Bride...

When we unpack it, intimacy can simply be described as 'into-me-see'. In other words, nothing held back, nothing hidden, no strings attached, conditions or requirements. No performance necessary - just unfailing acceptance and love. To experience love like that from the only One who has any right to judge us, yet doesn't because of Jesus, is a love that can't be lost, and a relationship worth giving your all for!

On one of our ministry trips, we were leading worship in a church in Swan Valley, Perth, and I was so overcome with love and gratitude for my Jesus, that I started to cry... during sound check! There wasn't a huge amount of atmosphere being created, no congregation in the auditorium, we were just running our songs for the service, but it took only one second to focus on Jesus, and see Him for who He is, and I was undone. He is delicious to me, beyond description - He's like a holy addiction, where a moment in His presence (and that doesn't need to be in a church service), leaves me so satisfied, yet so totally hungry for more!

God whispers...

There have been times when God has revealed Himself to me in the most vulnerable and sweet ways, that I'm completely changed by that one encounter. I remember one year, Equippers Church was hosting the annual conference for our church movement, and the guest speaker for the conference was Doctor Chris Hill. One evening, we had had a phenomenal service - prophetic and strong. The worship team was at another level - there was such an incredible sense of God's powerful presence there, and I was feeling all sorts of prophetic stirrings and faith declarations as I was leading. Pastor Chris ministered incredibly, and there was an amazing sense of ebb and flow between worship and word - he just kept taking it higher and further. After the service had finished, and most of the delegates had cleared the foyer, I realised I had left all my things backstage, so I went back into the darkened, empty theatre. As I walked past the curtain to the backstage area, I was overcome with a sense of God's presence still lingering there. Tears started to flow down my cheeks, and a little gasp left my lips as I whispered, *"You're still here."* Straight away, I felt God clearly, yet tenderly say, *"I didn't want to leave."* Now, of course I understand that God is omnipresent, but this was a very real sense of His manifest presence. That brush with His lingering, sweet, intimate presence, after all the power of the service had died down, was overwhelming, especially when I had a sense that He'd been waiting for me...

God in His entirety...

A couple of years ago, I sat down to have my devotions one morning after a busy few weeks where I hadn't really had any decent, one-on-one time with God. The date of my last journal entry had been more than a week before, and I felt that distance from Him. Coming from that place of perceived spiritual disconnection, I asked His forgiveness for not spending time, and I felt Him say *"You don't need to ask My forgiveness; you haven't done anything wrong. But you have made Me sad."* Because God longs for that time and connection with us, He feels the distance keenly, just as we do in any close human relationship, so it's possible for us to cause Him pain emotionally. We are, after all, made in His image with His DNA running through us, which is the only reason we have any capacity to love and be loved anyway.

But here's the thing - I believe we can't achieve true and complete intimacy until we begin to embrace Him for ALL He is, rather than just the parts of His character we understand and are most comfortable with. And again, it's a journey that God, in His graciousness, takes us on as we accept the invitation.

A tiny part of a very big story...

A few years ago I was in Sussex, England, staying with our dear friends Brent and Alex, having gone over to be with my sister Jilly, for the birth of her third son. I love England - I have already mentioned that I'm half British, and the first time I landed on UK soil, I felt like I was coming home. I also finally understood my Dad - growing up I thought he was kind of weird, but I realised he was actually just very British! And I loved that about him!

Anyway, during my time in England, my friend Sheridan and I spent the day in London, traipsing around the city, and visiting famous sights and landmarks. I adore the antiquity of England and Europe, especially as I live in a country that is very young. The primary school my kids attended boasts one of the oldest buildings in Auckland - a school house that dates back to about 1876! Yet, here I was in London seeing part of the Roman Wall that was 2000 years old - dating back to the time of Christ! There's something about antiquity that connects the wonder of the ancient past to the mystery of vast eternity, and makes you feel like a very tiny part of a very big story. And over, and under, and woven through all of this, is the supremacy and AWESOMENESS of Creator God!

Caught off guard...

On previous visits to London, I always felt very drawn to St Paul's Cathedral. A magnificent structure, this soaring cathedral has an enormous dome that makes the massive old oaks established in its grounds, look like tiny seedlings! And built for the glory of God! Although we know that church is not about a building, there is something about these mighty European cathedrals that does inspire a sense of reverence and awe! On a previous visit, as my friend Alex and I were walking through the grounds of St Paul's, we heard the strains of organ music coming from her interior, and something stirred deep in my spirit - it was like the building was calling to me, and I longed to be inside, listening up close, soaking up the atmosphere. Unfortunately, it was closed for the day as the organist rehearsed for the Sunday service.

But on this day in London, St Paul's was open, so Sheridan and I popped inside to have a look. I was excited to say the least! There were a number of people milling about, tourists interested in the way the cathedral was built, looking at her with an intense, yet purely architectural interest, while others sat quietly in the pews, waiting as 'evensong' was about to start. I took in every aspect of the atmosphere, especially as it had so stirred my spirit - the enormous height of the cathedral, the wonder at the dedication of those who built her, the cool, dim, yet peaceful interior, and even the pleasant, musty smell of a structure that was so old, and had seen so much worship, and so much tragedy, having barely survived the bombing of two World Wars. The story you could feel written in her walls was very sobering and very inspiring, and it was delightful to me in every way. I was not, however, prepared for what was about to happen. God was waiting to encounter me and reveal an aspect of His character that I was previously not even vaguely acquainted with!

Holiness and intimacy are linked...

I stood quietly near the back of the cathedral and started to feel strangely uncomfortable. I was struck by an awareness of myself and how very insignificant I was, as I became increasingly aware that I was in the Presence of something breathtakingly significant and eternal. And that Presence was weighty! I couldn't speak, there was a heavy hush in my heart, and I was overcome with something I had not encountered before - the absolute Holiness of God. All of a sudden, I knew I needed to be away from people, and it was all I could do to find a corner of the vast cathedral, and get on my knees, on the cold stone floor, with my hands over my head. I was so suddenly and keenly aware of whom I was - imperfect, sinful and human. And I began to weep. I was vaguely aware of the boy choir starting to sing, and the cathedral hauntingly and beautifully filling with the sound of their pure, sweet voices. But that was not the worship I was experiencing. As I wept, and felt such a strong connection to the imperfection of my humanity, I also felt the weight of His holiness, but, to my surprise and joy, it wasn't a fearsome, guilt-drenched feeling. More than anything, it was holiness, smothered in love! I had this overwhelming feeling that Almighty God could crush me like a bug, and would have every right to do so in my human state, yet, because of His enormous love for me, He wouldn't. He actually wanted to draw near to me! It was the clearest picture of the relationship between holiness and intimacy that I had ever experienced... and I felt new!

Fear is good...

I walked out of St Paul's Cathedral that day forever changed! I love the way a moment in His presence can completely rearrange our hearts for eternity! An aspect of God's character that I had never encountered before - awe and holiness - had been added to my understanding of Him. I began to understand what the Fear of the Lord meant! The Israelites, at the base of Mount Sinai, were

AFRAID of the manifestation of God, but had no FEAR of Him. The fear of the Lord can be a confusing concept because we automatically have a negative mindset when it comes to fear. As humans, because we haven't yet reached full understanding in so many areas, we have only our limited experience to draw on. So fear can be a negative thing, because of things we have encountered in our past based on a fallen world and sinful imperfect humanity. But there is a huge difference between fear and being afraid. There is a positive fear that grips our heart, and there is a negative fear that cripples our heart. And since the Bible says that perfect love casts out all fear, we conveniently throw out the whole concept of the fear of the Lord, as if His love for us cancels out the need to fear Him. In many cases in the Bible, the words for fear and worship are interchangeable, so some of our Biblical understanding of fear could just as easily be based on a mistranslation! I suggest that we need to get back to a healthy fear of the Lord, but to do so, we need to understand what fear in a healthy way really means.

The Webster Dictionary[4] defines fear as: *"having a reverential awe of (fear of) God."* It also says: *"fear is profound reverence and awe especially towards God."* It defines awe as: *"an emotion which combines dread, veneration and wonder, that is inspired by authority or by the sacred or sublime."* Reverence is defined as: *"honour or respect felt or shown; profound adoring, awed respect."* And wonder is: *"rapt attention or astonishment at something awesomely mysterious or new to one's experience."*

So, to paraphrase, having a fear of the Lord means to have profound reverence for Him, to feel reverential awe of Him, to be astonished at Him, and to have wonder in our hearts at His Mysteriousness. It means to be aware that He could totally wipe us out, and would have every right to do so, yet, at the same time, be absolutely amazed and astonished that He won't, because of His great love for us. Love that made a way to be loved in return, through Jesus' death on the Cross! When you spend a minute pondering that great thought, how can you not worship? How can you not rejoice? How can you not jump up and down and shout, at the top of your lungs: *"I AM LOVED! I AM FREE! THANK YOU JESUS!"*

Chapter Nine
My Soul Sings

"There's a sound that goes beyond melody and words and genre and style. A sound that is not about noise, volume, or even necessarily audible, but it is a sound of victory, promise, destiny, inheritance and abundance – a sound of hope, breakthrough, life and freedom. A prophetic utterance that comes from deep within the hearts of those who have committed to living what they sing every day."[1]

I am writing this sitting on the verandah of the little kauri cottage on our dear friend's farm in Otane, Hawkes Bay. It's a beautiful sunny, New Zealand summer day - a few wispy, light clouds, but a vast expanse of blue sky. A gentle breeze whispering through a huge beech tree about 100 metres away, sounds like the trickling water of a gentle stream. The roof of the cottage is creaking in the sun, and all around, especially when I close my eyes, I can hear the sounds of nature - a fly lazily buzzes by, various birds chatting, and the ever present and ever so iconic New Zealand sound of a cicada basking in the sun. A sparrow to my right sitting on the fence overlooking the hill, is chirping rhythmically and insistently before flying away, while to my left I can make out two or three different bird and insect chirps. As the breeze gets a little stronger, the beech tree is starting to intermittently sound like an appreciative crowd cheering at a rugby match...

Apart from one car that just drove down the dirt road a few kilometres away, and a distant cow mooing, one would think it's very quiet - there is no perceived NOISE, but there's a lot of sound that would be very easy to miss if I didn't choose to listen. Especially with my eyes closed...suddenly I'm hearing nature in magnificent surround-sound!

Heightened senses...

It's interesting that when one of our senses is dulled, or cut off completely, the others kick in more acutely. A blind person has heightened hearing, and the touch of their fingers becomes their eyes. The deaf rely greatly on their sight. When our sense of smell or touch is cut off, we can be in a dangerous place, especially if there's smoke or a hot element involved! I remember once, at Parachute Music Festival, trying to get to sleep in a noisy environment, so I climbed into bed with both ear plugs in, and an eye mask on. I woke up a few hours later unable to see or hear anything except my own internal heartbeat, and I wondered, for a split second in the dark, whether I had actually died and not quite made it to heaven!

The fact is our lives are filled up with so much constant NOISE, both visual and audible, that we can miss the important SOUND of life. One Christmas, my sister and brother-in-law with my nephews were in New Zealand from overseas, and we were away on holiday together. Josh and Gracie were around four and seven years of age at the time. One evening I was tucking my nephew Harry, who was three, into bed and he exclaimed to me, *"Every day I tell Gracie she's beautiful!"* I told Harry that that was a lovely thing to say, and asked what Gracie's response was, hoping she was treating her younger cousin kindly. He sighed an old-soul sigh as he said, *"She listens. But she doesn't hear me!"* Ahhhh, the wisdom of a three-year old! But it did get me thinking about the truth that it is possible to listen to noise, yet not truly hear the sound.

Noise or sound?

You see, I believe there is a huge difference between noise and sound. Our life can be very LOUD with noise, yet carry no weight of sound. Rob Bell, in his Nooma DVD entitled, *'Noise'2,* talks about the increase of noise filling our atmosphere, even in the last

20 years or so. Exponential increase that is actually quite scary, and we become accustomed to it without even realising it.

At the beginning of 2008, God took me on a journey that profoundly demonstrated this difference between noise and sound, and what my life carries. I probably shouldn't be surprised (yet I invariably am!) that when God speaks something into my heart, the enemy of my soul will usually combat that word with something altogether opposite in the natural. Our choice is always which voice we will listen to, and which word we will allow to shape and define us. I remember hearing our dear friend and mentor, Bishop Joseph Garlington, talking about his daughter who had a headache, and she was saying, *"My head hurts, my head hurts!"* to which he replied, *"Honey, don't say that. Say I believe I'm healed!"* So, in response, his daughter said, *"I believe I'm healed, I believe I'm healed… but my head still hurts!"* And Bishop Garlington said, it's not a contradiction, it's a statement of two realities, but one of them is going to overwhelm the other, if we just keep saying what God says!

So, at the beginning of 2008, I clearly felt God say it was a year to step out in greater authority and boldness in leading - both in worship leading, and in teaching and preaching. To be more bold in the areas of the prophetic realm. One would naturally assume that in order to worship-lead, preach and teach, one would require a voice. So, as I said, I shouldn't have been surprised that as I heard this from God, at the very same time I started having problems with my voice. I had had some degree of difficulty with my voice in the past, mostly through overuse and lack of technique, but nothing really significant or long lasting. However, this was clearly becoming an issue and heading towards vocal cord damage. I would lead worship in church on a Sunday, and completely lose my voice only two songs into the service. On top of that, my voice was taking days to recover, only to come right by the following Sunday, in time to repeat the process all over again!

I was on fire in my spirit, believing that God had spoken to me, ready to lead, and speak boldly and prophetically, but the very vehicle I needed to do that wasn't working properly. To say this was a little frustrating was a huge understatement. Yet, at the same time, there was a growing indignation, as I could sense the not-so-subtle ploy of the enemy to silence my voice, especially in light of what God had spoken to me.

What God says, goes...

From my observations and encounters with God over the years, it seems that God will speak in the spiritual realm and something is established at that level - God has said it, so it will be accomplished. This is why it is so important to really hear the voice and heart of the Holy Spirit in our everyday lives. Then the thing has to be established in the natural or physical realm and this is where the enemy comes in. Because he can't touch what God has spoken and established in the spiritual, he will try and wreak havoc in the natural. Our mistake, too often, is that we don't recognise the push-back for what it is, and we settle for what he tries to do, accepting it as simply 'natural'.

So in the midst of this situation, and in the face of what I believed God had spoken, I aligned myself and my thoughts with what God had said, and made the decision that His reality would overwhelm the current physical reality, as I declared truth and healing over my voice.

My voice got worse...

After a month of declaring, and praying, and believing, I decided that maybe a medical opinion might be a good idea, so off I trotted to an ENT specialist who stuck a camera down my throat and, matter-of-factly, told me I had a cyst in my vocal fold. The cyst was enlarged and, whether the vibrating of my cords was irritating the cyst and causing swelling, or whether the swollen cyst was causing the cords to not vibrate properly and cause greater strain, was indiscernible - chicken and egg stuff! But it was what it was, regardless.

I asked the specialist how I happened to have a cyst in my vocal fold and he was unhelpfully unclear - cysts are tricky things; he said it could even have been there from birth and just chosen now to appear, (how ironic!) But the bottom line was I would need vocal cord surgery under general anaesthetic, as a cyst would not heal up or disappear with vocal rest. He was intending to MAKE AN INCISION in my vocal fold and drain the cyst! Well, I can tell you, I was not overly enthused with the idea, and, although I left the appointment with a little more clarity, there was also a greater determination to align myself with what God said, not with what the physical symptoms and medical opinion presented to me! After all, in the grand scheme of things, a little cyst is not really a big deal for God, especially in the light of someone else believing Him for healing of an incurable disease - I figured a cyst was piecemeal to God.

Besides, He had spoken… so Wayne and I ramped up the prayer and faith efforts.

My voice got worse…

Hope deferred…

Three months down the track, we were heading into our annual Equippers Church Shout Conference, and I had a follow-up appointment with two specialists that day, before the opening night of the conference. We had been praying, and declaring, and 'yelling' in the spirit about my healing, and I went into the appointment fully believing that the specialist would look at my larynx, through the camera again, and exclaim in utter disbelief and awe that the cyst had disappeared! And I would proclaim, *"Hallelujah! God has healed me!"* and then proceed to lead everyone in the room to Jesus! So, when the specialist stuck the camera down my throat, conferred with the secondary specialist and said,

"Yep, the cyst is still evident. We will schedule the surgery", I was completely gutted - why had God not dealt with this silly little issue? He can heal cancer, why would He have difficulty with a cyst? Why would He miss a chance to be glorified? Why would He not heal me, especially in the light of what I'd felt Him say to me at the beginning of the year.

Well, I went into Shout Conference that evening, my vocal cords 'gave out' in the first service, and then I struggled through the rest of the time with barely any voice. It was an incredibly frustrating time - knowing you have this passion inside of you to lead people into God's presence, and sensing what He's saying and doing, but not being able to facilitate that. Maybe, just MAYBE, God was taking me down a different path and preparing to teach me something that I could not have learnt any other way. God is so good like that!

About six weeks later I was booked in for surgery. It was a very quick procedure where they cut an incision in the vocal fold, drained the cyst (multiple cysts as it turned out), and then left the little flap of the vocal fold to reconnect and heal itself. Now, when one is dealing with one's very tender vocal folds and cutting them open with very sharp instruments, there's a fair amount of uncertainty and trepidation involved. One is inclined to pray that the surgeon did not have a little too much wine with dinner the night before! What terrified me more, however, was the fact that after the surgery, I would be required to be silent for ten days! TEN DAYS! Of COMPLETE silence! No talking, no whispering, no laughing, no singing, no worshipping - no communication in the way that I am used to communicating! Needless to say, I was not too thrilled about this, but I had no choice but to embrace the journey…

Be still my soul…

There's something about silence that stills your soul. Even though there was the hum of a busy house around me when I got home from the hospital, the simple fact that I wasn't able to physically contribute to that noise, brought a very stilling effect to my soul. I felt more calm (that could have partly been the drugs!) and, overall, just a stillness in my heart. I do wonder if, with the mounting volume of noise in our atmosphere, there comes an anxiety and urgency almost, to have a voice, to be heard, and to contribute? With that pressure taken off, and with the deliberation it took to write down what I needed to communicate with my family, everything within me felt more relaxed and calm. There's something to be said for King David telling his soul to be quiet and at rest!

Be still my mouth!

This led to the realisation, and rather sad acceptance, that I had been putting a whole lot of mindless noise into the atmosphere around my life, and others' lives, in the form of useless words, which carried no weight whatsoever. A whole lot of fluffy nonsense that mattered nothing, but just messed up the atmosphere. For you women reading this, we don't HAVE to use up the 20,000 words supposedly allotted to us per day. Most of it is just noise pollution anyway! As I mentioned in chapter six, one of my favourite, and possibly most challenging scriptures, is Proverbs 18:18.

"Words kill; words give life. They're either poison or fruit. You choose!" (MSG)

So, I made a decision that when I could speak again, I wanted to speak words that gave life, that were creative, not destructive, and that were weighty with purpose.

The next thing I realised was that I was beginning to relish this quietness - it was like a refuge in the midst of the chaos of everyday life. Again, because there was no pressure to be heard or to have a voice, this still place became like an oasis I could escape to. And wonders will never cease, as I quietened my soul, all of a sudden I was hearing God a whole lot more easily, and with greater clarity. And then it hit me, I could 'hear' songs in my soul! There was constantly a song and music going round in my spirit - it wasn't physically audible, obviously, but it was as if my soul was singing continually! It just took a different sense, and silence, to 'hear' it!

Worship is more than a song...

I have known for many years that worship comes from the heart. I have preached for many years that worship comes from the heart. This was a revelation to me in my teenage years because, before that, worship to me was standing up in church, with a hymnal and singing a hymn, while the organ played. And I felt no connection with God when I sang those hymns, even though they were beautifully written, and the stories behind many of them were incredibly powerful. The problem was with me, not the hymns, because, as a teenager, I hadn't yet learnt what worship truly was.

Again, I think Bishop Joseph Garlington put it brilliantly, when he wrote: *"Worship is to act as an inferior before a superior."* How crazy to think that singing beautifully and playing masterfully is going to be an acceptable worship offering to God, in and of itself. Does this disqualify the tone deaf from worshipping? If someone sings a little off key, does God put His hands over His ears and wince as He sends them away, telling them to get singing lessons first before they can come back and worship Him? Seriously?

Now, I am all for singing and playing beautifully - I have quoted Chronicles many times when working with church music teams - there were 288 MASTER musicians leading the worship in David's Tabernacle. But are we really so shallow-minded to think that if we simply sing and play beautifully, but our heart is not engaged, then that is going to be pleasing to God? We still, too often, confuse worship with music. It is possible to sing the latest God-song perfectly in tune, with all the vocal trills and thrills, and it's a beautiful NOISE, but the SOUND your life is making is altogether different! This is NOT worship!

So, as I said, I knew that worship comes from the heart. I knew it in my head, but I was blindly arrogant enough to think I really understood what that meant. And it wasn't until the NOISE of worship was stripped away from me, that I realised that I still placed too much stock in the songs, the words, the melodies, the arrangements, and the way the worship made ME feel!

Noiseless, yet loud worship...

So, the Sunday morning after my surgery, I stood on the front row of church, and I made a decision to worship in the place of silence. But it wasn't quiet, reflective worship as my situation probably dictated, and, as would have been convenient for me. I raised my hands, I jumped and danced, I mouthed all the words, I engaged my heart. AND MY SOUL SANG! To all intents and purposes, to someone looking on, I was worshipping with everything in me. There was no noise coming out of my mouth, but there was a sound of worship that was rising up from a new, deeper place that I had never experienced before. I was not bound by the limitations of noise - I felt free! And to this day, it is still one of the most powerful worship times I have ever experienced!

In the midst of these ten silent days, I wrote this song:

"Words are not enough, to describe the majesty of God
There's a sound of worship, rising up from deep within my heart
In the place of silence, I will find a way to praise You
To praise You still
It's a new place, from a new heart, it's a new day...
My soul sings, my soul sings
As I reach to God-Alive
Beyond the words, beyond the songs
My soul sings
    I will be still, and know, You are God

I will be still, and know, You are God"
- 'My Soul Sings' 3

God answers with a question...

And then came day eight of the journey. I was probably at my most vulnerable at this point. I had been pressing into God in my quiet times, relishing all He was showing me, and actually loving the journey, but this day I was feeling worried. What if my voice didn't come back? I had slipped up twice in the few days, and spoken out a word or two without thinking. What if the flap had dislodged and not healed properly damaging my cords irreparably. But mostly, I was thinking about the call of God, and the word He had spoken to me at the beginning of the year, and whether I would be able to fulfil that.

And I asked God the question:

"Father, what if I can't sing again?"

Now please hear me, I really don't care about singing - as I mentioned in an earlier chapter, God dealt with that in me long ago as a teenager, when I did unknowingly at the time, get a lot of worth from singing. Worth from something I could do rather than finding my worth in just being in Him. So, this question was not about physically singing, it was about the passion and desire in my heart to facilitate the call of God on my life... and I needed a voice to do that.

Have you ever heard God answer a question, with a question of His own? He has done that to me on a few occasions and it's kind of frustrating! What I was wanting to hear from Him was: *"I've healed you!"* Or, *"Trust Me, I've done it all!"* or something comforting and assuring of that nature. But God simply answered me with a question:

"Then, My daughter, will you still sing?"

What sort of crazy contradiction was this? I wanted to hear assurance that everything would be fine, but God was challenging me to think differently. Otherwise what was this whole journey for? In essence, God was saying to me:

"Even if you never get your voice back again, will you still 'sing'? Will everything about the WAY you live your life be a song to me? Will everything about your life message be LOUD, whether you ever utter an audible sound again or not?"

Your life sings your loudest message...

This is, in essence, a large part of my life message. What sound resonates from my life? What does my life shout the loudest? Because it is possible to say one thing, but be totally living another. It's even possible to declare some things in faith with the right intentions, but, unless our concepts, and precepts, and thought-processes have been aligned with the heart and the Word of our Father, our life will be singing two different melodies. Will my life sing defeat or victory? Will my life sing depression or joy? Anxiety or peace? Lack or abundance? Self-accomplishment or self-surrender? Pride or humility? Self-awareness or God-awareness? Bondage or freedom? I can SAY I want to live those good things, and even declare that I am, but if my mind isn't renewed and challenged, my mouth will surely start to undo those declarations, and my day-to-day actions won't be far behind!

Be assured, though, as I stated at the beginning of this book, life is an invitation to a journey. If you simply make a decision to love God with ALL your heart, and then love people as much as you love yourself, then you're on the right track! The heart of the Father is to work in us the likeness of His Son, and to bring us into an intimate relationship with Him, where we are fully surrendered, yet fully alive at the same time. And this has nothing to do with what we can DO for Him, it's all about who we ARE in His presence.

John Eldredge said,

"The glory of God is man, fully alive!"4

I can think of no greater way to be fully alive than knowing God's heart towards me, and knowing He's got it all sussed. There's absolute freedom in walking in the peace and security that that knowledge brings!

God has set everything straight...

To finish the story, at the end of the ten days of silence, I did get my voice back (it sounded very wispy and odd at first), although I wasn't able to sing for another month. At the end of that month, I read a verse in Psalms 97 that said:

"Daughters of Zion, sing your hearts out; God has done it all, has set everything straight!" (MSG)

And I knew it was a rhema word from God for me. I thought I had needed to hear that in the midst of the journey, but God knew He needed to teach me something that went a lot deeper than the physical situation. This scripture became my confession and my declaration. Five months later, the specialist spoke to me and said he didn't think my voice sounded like it had recovered as well as it should have. He asked me to come in and see him again, looked down my throat with the camera and told me that the cysts had all re-filled, and I would need to have surgery again. That news, second time around, held no shock or fear for me. I knew surgery was not the path God had for me this time. He had given me my word, and I was standing on it.

That day, the specialist put me on the hospital waiting list. And to THIS day, I have never heard from him again and there has been no contact from the hospital with a scheduled surgery time. It's as if I just fell off the grid. I believe God has healed me, and I have steadily been leading worship at church every week when I'm home, and in many churches around New Zealand and the world, recording, and teaching, and preaching. Apart from getting sick, my voice never fails me, but it keeps getting stronger, as I have clung to what I believed God showed me, and just kept walking the journey He has me on.

The journey is the destination...

But that's what the life-journey with God is often like. As I've already said, it's always more about the journey than the destination! There's all this 'stuff' that goes on in the natural, at surface level, but underneath it all, God is wanting to use that to take us deeper, train us, and teach us a new reality. I fully believed God would heal me in the beginning, but He didn't. So I walked the journey God needed me to walk, and, only then, did He give me my rhema word about the external situation. God spoke to me at the beginning of that year about greater boldness in leading - both worship leading and teaching - and also preaching in prophetic boldness. I was naive enough to think I only required a voice to do that. I'm so thankful that God took me on the journey, and taught me it was my LIFE that needed to shout loudest!

Chapter Ten
Living Building Stones...

"All this energy issues from Christ: God raised Him from death and set Him on a throne in deep heaven, in charge of running the Universe, everything from galaxies to governments, no name and no power exempt from His rule. And not just for the time being, but forever. He is in charge of it all, has the final word on everything. At the centre of all this, Christ rules the church. The Church you see, is not peripheral to the world; the world is peripheral to the Church. The Church is Christ's body, in which He speaks and acts, by which He fills everything with His power." (Ephesians 1:20-23 MSG)

I absolutely love this passage in Ephesians. It paints the most amazing picture of Jesus, ruling EVERYTHING! The magnitude and sovereignty of His rule and dominion is extremely hard to fathom. When He was resurrected, He had conquered all and He took His rightful place as King - no name or power exempt from His rule. And at the very centre of it all, Christ rules the Church.

The Church - God's answer to a lost and hurting world. Not a building or physical structure, nor based on form and formula, and therefore constantly prone to cultural changes, but a body of people. Living, breathing stones that Jesus is building into His body, of whom He is the head, and where the Holy Spirit is so very welcome.

We are the Church! I am the Church! You are the Church! Look at this passage from Ephesians 2:20-22:

"God is building a home. He's using us all - irrespective of how we got here - in what He is building. He used the apostles and prophets for the foundation. Now He's using you, fitting you in brick by brick, stone by stone, with Christ Jesus as the cornerstone that holds all the parts together. We see it taking shape day after day - a holy Temple built by God, all of us built into it, a Temple in which God is quite at home." (MSG)

Which leads us to ask these questions: Why? And what? Why would God use me to be part of the Church? And what does that look like? Couldn't church just be something I attend on Sunday, pay my tithes, tick the God-box, and then be done with for the week? Does the Church really demand more of my life? Well, that really depends on how you view your life and its purpose, doesn't it? You're either living for yourself and your own desires, or you're living for a higher cause - to love God, and to love people.

Then you might say, *"Well, I show God I love Him by going to church on Sunday!"* And my response would be, *"Awesome! Now how does your going to church on Sunday affect the rest of your week, in the way you love people?"* Because that is what it comes down to. We, as the Church, are the answer to pain, loneliness, brokenness, poverty, injustice, sickness, and every other condition or situation that arises from the situation of sin! And that happens outside the walls of the structure we define as church. It happens as we ARE the Church to the world around us!

Seven year-old wisdom...

A number of years ago, I was picking my son Josh up from school, and, as we drove home, we had the radio playing. Wayne and I were still in the Parachute Band, and we were leaving that evening for another three week American tour. As we were listening, a song came on the radio with the lyrics, 'I can't wait to get to heaven'. Josh, who was seven years old at the time, sighed as he echoed the words of the song out loud, *"I can't wait to get to heaven."* My response started a conversation that ended with me being utterly dumbfounded.

"Why can't you wait to get to heaven, buddy?"

"Oh, because there's no sadness in Heaven, and no stress, and I'll get to play with my friends all day," he replied.

"You're right," I said, *"There's no sadness in heaven, because all sadness is caused by sin!"*

"No it's not." Josh countered.

"Yes it is, buddy. Every sort of sadness we feel, can be traced somehow back to sin - sickness, hurt, grief - everything goes back to the fact that sin entered the world, and messed everything up. And sinful people, without Jesus, have stayed in that messed up place, and kept living it out, hurting themselves and others."

And then came his response...

"But the sadness I feel when you go on tour isn't caused by sin, in fact it's caused by the exact opposite of sin. You and Daddy are going away to bring people closer to Jesus... and that's the exact opposite of sin!"

I had no comeback. The profundity of his seven-year old mind blew me away. Mind you, this was the same boy who, at four years of age, during communion at church, called out in a very loud voice, *"Hooray! Here come the drinks!"*

But what he had grasped at seven was a deep truth. It wasn't expressed with a hint of manipulation or 'poor me' attitude attached. Although he probably didn't realise the depth of the concept, he had basically summed up this reality: *'There's a hurt, broken and needy world out there, and we carry the answer to their brokenness.'*

Words without backing...

St Francis of Assisi said:

"Preach the Gospel at all times, and when necessary, use words!"

How much damage has been done in the name of Christ, where people have preached the Gospel, but their lives have been preaching an altogether different message? Religion lives and breathes in that place. A whole lot of words, laws and requirements, yet no requirement of a holy life lived to back those words up. Only relationship demands that sort of life. A love-relationship with the One who rules over all, is supreme over all, and chooses to live INSIDE of us! His Church! His living, breathing, no-walls, limitless Church!

If we continue to think of church as just a building, an establishment, a social centre, or even just a place to worship on Sunday, we will be buying into religion - religion that can do nothing to change our hearts, but actually binds us up. But when we see Church as a body of people, reflecting the life and love of Jesus, filled with the power of the Holy Spirit, commissioned to change their world, then we're onto something powerful. I don't know about you, but I WANT TO BE THE CHURCH!

Hurt people, hurt people. Chained people, chain people. Broken people, break people. But free people, free people! Changed people, change people! Those who have been forgiven much, forgive and love much. All of this is birthed in the RELATIONSHIP we have with Jesus. When we begin to truly realise that the same power that raised Jesus from the dead, now lives in us, we're unstoppable!

The Kingdom of God walks in...

In Proverbs 21:22 it says this:

"One sage, entered a whole city of armed soldiers - their trusted defences fell to pieces." (MSG)

What would cause a whole city of armed soldiers, to drop their weapons, and run for cover? What could disarm the defences of a city like that, causing them to completely fall to pieces? The recognition that a greater power and authority has just entered the atmosphere, that's what. When the Kingdom of God walks in, the enemy flees. And how does the Kingdom of God walk into the atmosphere of the world? Not through a church building, or the right formula of church service, but through the Church made of living stones - you and me. We carry His Kingdom wherever we go, and while we do whatever we do. That knowledge should make us think a little more carefully about our decisions, directions and actions! Carry His Kingdom boldly, carry His Kingdom gloriously, carry His Kingdom honourably!

Atmosphere shifters...

We have been called to be atmosphere-changers. It should be normal for you, as a Christian, to walk into any environment, and the atmosphere shifts simply because you've entered it. And not because you, in your own strength, have that ability but, because the Shifter of Atmospheres has walked in, inside of you! Phew! That takes the pressure off somewhat, doesn't it? Just be the living, breathing Church, and carry Jesus well, with confidence and authority - that's all you have to do!

Bill Johnson tells the story of an organic shop he liked to visit which was owned and operated by some new-age followers. He liked to browse around the aisles of the shop, because he enjoyed their produce, but could sense the spiritual atmosphere inside, so before he would enter the shop, he would stand outside the door and pray, and wait until he felt God's presence strongly with him. As he focused on Jesus, and stilled his own conscious clamouring, he would feel God's presence with him, and then he would walk into the shop. One day the owner of the shop came up to Bill and said to him, *"You know Bill, we really love it when you come into our shop."* Upon asking why, the owner answered Bill, *"Because when you walk in, the atmosphere changes!"*

Any atmosphere should shift when we walk into it because we carry the Kingdom of God within us.

After the release of his album, 'Love God, Love People'[1] Israel Houghton had the opportunity to perform one of his songs on the

'Jay Leno Live' show. He didn't say a word, there wasn't even an interview, but Jay Leno watched him as he left the stage, and commented, *"There's something about that guy!"*

The atmosphere around our lives should be such that people notice something different in us, without us needing to even utter a word.

Obey the signs…

And what it basically comes down to is this: Authority. I would have a poor show of standing in the middle of the street and directing traffic, if I wasn't wearing a policeman's uniform. I could use all the right hand signals and blow a whistle, yet I would have no authority, and would be more likely to be bowled by the traffic. But as soon as a policeman steps onto the scene, the drivers obey. Why? Because they recognise the authority that has been given to that policeman - unless they are rebels with a senseless cause, they will obey simply because of the recognition of that authority.

One recent summer evening, Wayne, Gracie, Josh and I went out to the beach to build a bonfire with the aim of cooking sausages and toasting marshmallows. When we arrived, there was a sign saying 'Total Fire Ban', but because we had built a fire there the previous summer, we assumed it was a recent enforcement that only applied to the reserve and camping ground, not the actual beach. We built the mound of firewood, and had brought some coal from home. Wayne built the fire from our gathered driftwood, and it was touch and go for while, especially when we realised we had no paper and the coal required being soaked in lighter fluid first, but, after about half a box of matches, he got the fire cranking. We even got a few marshmallows toasted, and were just about to 'incinerate the snarlers', when a lady approached on a four-wheeler bike and told us we needed to put the fire out. She wasn't particularly scary or formidable, and it was obvious she was just a public citizen, but we recognised her authority, (not just when she showed us her hi-vis helmet!) but mostly when she mentioned her 'connections' to the fire service and the $400 fine that would be applied if we didn't put the fire out immediately! She didn't have to force us, and, in fact, she was very pleasant and almost apologetic, but she carried a connection to a greater authority and we recognised that.

Whether you feel or look powerful or not is of no account. The authority and power of Jesus' Name lives in you, therefore you have all the power and authority of heaven behind you! The devil recognises the authority you carry in the Name of Jesus, and he will do whatever he can to keep you from recognising that authority in yourself, but all his schemes can't negate the Truth - you just have to believe it and walk in it!

Impacted but not yet transformed...

Obviously we have Biblical account and, therefore, the revelation of the supreme authority of Jesus as Messiah, to confirm this to us. I am so glad to be living in the time that we are, with the complete Word of God to guide and lead us - we have the whole picture from beginning to end. But imagine how the disciples felt at the foundation of the establishment of the early Church. They had lived with Jesus for three years - they'd walked, talked, eaten, laughed and ministered with Him for THREE YEARS! Jesus, in the flesh! They saw Him do incredible miracles - healings, deliverances, resurrections, multiplications and transformations - and they even got a chance to do a few miracles themselves. They knew enough about Jewish culture and law to recognise and honour Jesus as Rabbi, although, because they were basically tradesmen, they would never have qualified as disciples themselves. Perhaps that's why they followed so willingly - aware they would never have 'made the grade' - yet this man, who was so very different, seemed to accept and believe in them. They even had the odd glimpse of who He really was, and yet even up to His death on the Cross, and then Resurrection, they were still a rag-tag bunch of society's misfits - living with Jesus had touched them...

but they were not yet changed.

Living with Jesus wasn't enough alone to transform them. Seeing His miracles wasn't enough alone to transform them. Even experiencing and operating in the miraculous themselves, was not enough alone to transform them. These things were enough to amaze them, and induce their loyalty, but not to transform them completely.

So what made the difference? Somewhere between Peter the fisherman, denying Jesus the night before His death, and Peter the Apostle, powerfully preaching the gospel, something happened. And that something is the foundation of the Church, the foundation for our lives, and the foundation of the authority we now carry.

Revelation demands worship...

During the 40 days after His resurrection, Jesus appeared to the disciples in many different configurations. He walked with two on the road to Emmaus, and talked with them, until their eyes were opened to who He was. He relieved Peter's heart of the guilt of his desertion, while cooking him fish on the beach for breakfast. And He dispelled Thomas' doubt by allowing him to touch the nail scars in his hands. He met with them, and ate with them, and told them many things, most importantly, that they were to wait in Jerusalem for power to come.

And finally, Jesus had told them to meet Him on the Mount of Olives, and the Bible says in Matthew 28 that, *"the moment they SAW Him, they worshipped Him."* The only other mention of Him being worshipped after His resurrection, was when He showed Himself to the women at the tomb, and upon revelation of who He was, they fell at His feet and worshipped. It may just be my supposition, but I like to think that Jesus showed Himself to the disciples in different ways during the 40 days, but He fully revealed Himself, right before His final ascension, on the Mount of Olives. And when they SAW Him as Lord and Messiah, they WOR-

SHIPPED Him!

It's interesting to reflect on that little note at the end of verse 17, too, *"...but some doubted."* I have often wondered why this was added in to this Scripture, and I can only come to the conclusion that the kindness of God makes provision in our weakness. Maybe these ones became stronger in their faith and worship, because of the presence of doubt? Even if your natural mind tends to veer more towards doubt, worship Jesus regardless! Full faith is on its way! When Jesus fully reveals Himself to us, our only reasonable response is WORSHIP! Even when our natural mind can't make sense of it...

Come, Holy Spirit...

And then Jesus gave them their final instructions:

"All authority in heaven and on earth has been given to me. Therefore go and make disciples of all nations, baptising them in the name of the Father and of the Son and of the Holy Spirit, and teaching them to obey everything I have commanded you. And surely I am with you always, to the very end of the age." (Matthew 28:18-20 NIV)

So, the disciples did as Jesus instructed, and waited in Jerusalem. He had told them He would be with them to the end of the age, and so they waited for the promise of this endless presence in the form of the Holy Spirit! And when He came, they were instantly transformed. You see they had lived WITH Jesus, but now Jesus was living IN them. That was the difference. That's what transformed the fisherman into the apostle. That's how the church was birthed - in the true revelation and acceptance of Jesus as Messiah, in worship, and in the power of the indwelling Holy Spirit. That's what will transform you - you are the Church!

Change your world...

And the world around you, YOUR world, needs to be able to see that. We need to be those who can walk into any situation, any atmosphere, and see it shift and change, because the Kingdom of God has just walked in, INSIDE us! I love especially the first few chapters of the book of Acts, as we see the result of the disciples and followers of Jesus being filled with the Holy Spirit. Any outward display of the Holy Spirit's power should cause a reaction! When the disciples and followers all began speaking in tongues, the people's response was a confused, *"What's going on here?"* And then Peter, yes Peter the uneducated, unschooled, rough-around-the-edges fisherman, began to speak out boldly - now a public preacher, unpacking the prophecies in Scripture, and tying it all together like a trained professional! And that same day 3000 people were added to the Kingdom! This was radical, life-changing, nation-shaking stuff!

Then we read an account of Peter and John being thrown into prison because of their preaching and the miraculous healing of a lame beggar. The next morning they were brought out before all the religious leaders and rulers, who were completely threatened by these 'religious rebels', and asked to explain themselves. Peter, full of the Holy Spirit, again began to preach boldly, declaring Jesus' death and resurrection, and the religious leaders could hardly believe what they were hearing. The boldness and confidence of these men, who were obviously unschooled, with no formal Scriptural training, flabbergasted them. These men had been with Jesus, but this was a whole new level of authority and boldness, and they couldn't comprehend it, but they knew they couldn't let it get out of hand. Already the followers had grown to at least 5000 people. Revival was breaking out in opposition to everything they taught and held the people bound with!

Church alive!

Miraculous healing and deliverances were taking place, and

people were being baptised and choosing to freely follow this rebel group of Jesus' disciples. This 'Church' was alive, and encouraging a whole different sort of law, than what the priests and religious leaders were teaching. Freedom and liberty, joy and life were flowing. There was incredible unity - people living in community and sharing everything they had and everything they did. They were holding regular 'church meetings' on the porch of Solomon's Temple, and daily, people were being added to their number. Sick and infirm were being laid in the streets and Peter's SHADOW started healing them! People from all the surrounding villages of Jerusalem started pouring into the city bringing their sick, and Acts 5:16 says ALL were healed!

The religious leaders were enraged and threw the Apostles into jail again. As if a man-made prison could contain the power of the Church! And an angel came in the night and released them, leading them out without even unlocking the cells. When they were called for the next morning, the officials found the prison locked up tight, with the guards still stationed outside the doors, and the disciples were already at it again, preaching at the Temple. And again, this time the chief of the Temple police, and the high priests all exclaimed: *"What's going on here, anyway?"*

This is movie-material!

I would love to see a movie made about the Book of Acts! This is heady, powerful, exciting stuff. Imagine what the 6 o'clock News would look like if even this story of the jail escape was being reported today? *'Prison Break'?* would pale in comparison. We can read these accounts in Acts in a ho-hum sort of manner, but it's all true - it actually happened. This was all part of the establishment of the Church - birthed in worship and the power of the Holy Spirit, operating through common men, who dared to live boldly for Jesus. Unity, community, worship, the powerful preaching of the Word, freedom and the power of the Holy Spirit were all hallmark, foundational features of the early Church. And the obvious spin-off of this in-filling of the Holy Spirit was freedom, changed lives, unity and revival breaking out - sounds like something that shifts an atmosphere. Sounds like something that could change a nation...

I am the Church, you are the Church...

God's intention to use us as living, building stones, to build His Church hasn't changed, so when did church suddenly become just a building we go to on Sunday? Remember what Ephesians 1 says: *"...at the centre of all this, Christ rules the Church. The Church you see, is not peripheral to the world: the world is peripheral to the Church."* When did the Church suddenly start trailing behind, trying to fit into the culture of the day and be relevant, when God called the Church to be counter-cultural and radically different?

As Bishop Mark Chironna says:

"You can't transform the culture by catering to the culture; you can only transform the culture by introducing a greater, more powerful culture that has the ability to transform lives!" [4]

That's the Kingdom of God operating in and through us. And that's the Church I want to be a living, breathing part of!

My question is are we doing it? Are we letting God have His way with us so that we are so filled with His presence, so sure of His purpose and so soaked in His Word, that the atmosphere changes when we walk into it? Are we aware that all authority is ours to change our world, because it has been given to us, whether we feel powerful or not? And this isn't just the mandate for pastors, preachers and full-time ministers. This is for all of us. Are we living CHANGE? Are we living FREEDOM? Are we living UNITY and REVIVAL? Ultimately, are we living lives that cause those around us to ask, *"What's going on here? There's something different about you..."*

Chapter 11
It's All About Jesus

"Jesus at the centre of it all, Jesus at the centre of it all
From beginning to the end
It will always be
It's always been You, Jesus, Jesus
Nothing else matters, nothing in this world will do
Jesus You're the centre, and everything revolves around You
Jesus You
>From my heart, to the Heavens,
>Jesus be the centre
>It's all about You, yes it's all about You
Jesus be the centre of Your Church, Jesus be the centre of Your Church
Every knee will bow, and every tongue shall confess You Jesus"

- 'Jesus at the Centre'[1]

One of the greatest privileges Wayne and I have, apart from being involved in our own team at Equippers Church, and running Equippers Creative Lab[2] in Auckland, is the chance to be able to visit so many other churches, both in New Zealand and in many nations around the world. Recently, we were in nine different nations in just over two months. Very different cultures, very different languages, very different landscapes, very different climates. Apart from the visual and sensory overload, (one day we were standing at the base of the Petronas Towers in the muggy heat of Kuala Lumpur, Malaysia, and four days later we were climbing up Mt Pilatus in the sunny chill of Lucerne, Switzerland), the overriding impression we have been left with is that Jesus is establishing Himself at the very centre of His Church. Cultural preferences, language, personality, and communication styles aside, it's all about Jesus, and His Kingdom, and nothing else.

We have all seen different moves of the Holy Spirit where incredible things happen - things difficult for the natural mind to comprehend - and these moves have been very genuine, until man seems to latch onto the physical manifestations of the Spirit as the focus, and the centrality of Jesus is forgotten. The Holy Spirit was never meant to be glorified - even in the establishment of the early Church, where crazy, miraculous things were happening, the power of Jesus' death and resurrection was continually being preached as the main thing. I am willing to stand corrected, but I believe that one of the Holy Spirit's main functions is to glorify Jesus - when we simply, yet boldly lift Jesus up, the Holy Spirit has freedom to move. A genuine exalting of Jesus should make way for the power and presence of the Holy Spirit.

Linear or circular?

I used to think it a noble and right thing to tell Jesus that He was first in my life, and everything fell into place beneath Him. But even the fact that I think of a linear list, would suggest that the further down that list I go, the less importance and priority I place on those things. We can subtly begin to think that there are certain areas that we don't need to 'bother' Jesus with. Certain things in our lives that we assume He doesn't really have an interest in, or really even need to have a say about, especially as He's so busy running the Universe! But what if He doesn't want to be right at the top of my long list of priorities? What if He doesn't want merely a linear relationship with me and my priorities, but a circular one? What if He wants to be right slap-bang in the middle of the glorious mess of my everyday life? What if He wants to be fully involved - His grace and mercy and guidance, touching and interacting with EVERY part of my heart and my world?

You see, it's easy to think we are putting Jesus first, and yet we're not allowing Him to actually affect the different compartments of our lives. What if He wants to be at the centre, with everything else revolving around Him? That would certainly change the way I view EVERYTHING. When He's at the centre, He gets to relate to and speak into every part of me - my relationships, my finances, my workplace, my lifestyle, my purpose, my conversations, my thoughts, my emotions, the way I spend my time, who I spend it with! Everything looks different with Jesus at the centre...

The centrality of Jesus...

More than anything that's what I'm sensing God is calling us back to: the simplicity of the centrality of Jesus. Totally, completely. Both in the Church and individually, although obviously if we get this right individually, then we get it right as the Church too. For too long we have made things too complicated, and as this world is spinning more and more towards crazy point - the pace of life is hectic, technology is developing at an alarming rate, that we can't really predict what's around the corner, even in the next few years - we need to keep it strong and simple. It's all about Jesus - He hasn't changed, His purposes stand, and more than ever, we need to lift Him up and stand on His Word.

The Bridegroom and His Bride...

Jesus is coming back soon - I'm more convinced of it now than ever before. I feel it, I sense it in the atmosphere, and I'm hearing it echoed in others' hearts, and coming out in their conversations. And the beautiful thing is, He's coming back for His Bride, His wife. He's not coming back for a business associate, or for a servant, or even a minister. He's not coming back for a worship leader or a preacher. He's coming back for the love of His life - the bride He is passionately in love with, and He wants her to be passionately in love with Him! He doesn't want a bride who professes her love on Sunday, but then 'prostitutes' herself with other 'loves' throughout the week. Again, it's easy to say, *"That would NEVER be me! I love God with all my heart, soul, mind and strength!"* yet the way we spend our time, our money and the things we dwell on in our thoughts - the things that fill our head space - will contradict our confession! If you really want to know what you love and worship, just take a mental inventory of those three things - your time, your money and your thoughts - and you'll recognise your 'god', and at which altar you are worshipping!

In the words of Ross King, in his incredibly challenging song, 'Clear the Stage',

"Anything I put before my God, is an idol.
Anything I want with all my heart, is an Idol.
Anything I can't stop thinking of, is an idol.
Anything that I give all my heart, is an idol."[3]

Warts and all...

When Wayne and I got married, he married ME - he didn't marry my abilities (of which there are many I might add!) He didn't even marry the future promise of what I might become. He loved and married ME as I was then. I didn't marry a phenomenal musician, a singer, worship leader and a preacher. I loved and married Wayne as He was then. Don't get me wrong, he is all of those things, but that's not WHO I married. We dreamed about being in ministry and serving God together, and we knew that was our calling, but that's not why we got married. It didn't just seem like a convenient arrangement, or a chance to outwork our giftings together. We were best friends, our hearts were knitted together in God, and we just could not foresee a future without each other in it! We were in love! And because that has been our foundation for marriage, we have had the crazy, fun ride of accessing all the rest of the 'stuff' we can DO as we serve God together in ministry! Heart came first, purpose came second!

Believe it or not, Jesus doesn't want you for your skill set - He just wants you for YOU. As I look back on my own salvation experience, I realise that the Holy Spirit didn't just get involved once I'd given my heart to Jesus, but He was there all along, wooing and drawing me - almost courting me you could say - until I was ready to accept His 'marriage proposal'. And guess what - He proposed when I was at my lowest, most vulnerable state, and He has kept confirming that betrothal over and over, throughout the journey of my life. He hasn't been waiting for me to get a whole lot of things figured out first. He's not waiting for you to get your act together or up-skill before He'll propose - His very invitation to relationship is like the wedding proposal, and if you'll look back on your journey, He didn't wait until you'd got it all together, before that invitation came! He wants you for you, warts and all.

There's a reason that God uses the marriage analogy to describe His relationship with His Church, and there's also a reason that the enemy so viciously attacks and undermines the sanctity and preciousness of the marriage relationship. Because marriage is the ultimate reflection, on this earth, of the intimacy we are to share with God, but also the partnership in ruling that we were created for. God didn't just make us so He could save us from the desperate state we'd managed to get ourselves into. His original intent was that we would live in unbroken fellowship with Him - an intimate close relationship. So He had to save us to bring us back to that relationship - how sad that many never choose to take that step towards Him, but are satisfied with living this temporal, earthly existence their own way, with a ticket to heaven thrown in at the end!

The plan has always been intimacy...

I believe everything in the spiritual realm has a counterpart in the natural, which is the outworking or reflection of that spiritual principle. Marriage is the exact representation of what God intends in our relationship with Him. The enemy knows that, and so will do anything in his power to stop people seeing and finding that intimacy for themselves! If he can blur the lines, and confuse and blind people to the truth, even in the natural, he has at least won some souls on this planet. What an absolute tragedy.

The other tragedy is that we get so busy doing things FOR God, as a poor substitute for relationship WITH Him. But God wants the Church for her heart first, not for what she can do for Him. We run the risk of putting so much time and effort into our programmes, relevant ministries and services, that we can lose His heart. Don't get me wrong, these are all important and we need to be reaching the lost, obviously, but not without the foundation of our heart for Jesus. Otherwise we run the risk of becoming like the Ephesian Church, in Revelation 2. God spoke to her and commended her for all the good things she was doing, her faithfulness in serving Him and not tolerating evil, but you can hear the pain in His heart when He tells her that she has lost her first love for Him. And that loss of first-heart love was enough to have her candlestick potentially removed from among the churches.

Marriage rights...

Marriage, as I realised the morning after our wedding, when I tangibly sensed God's smile on us as a couple, is about intimacy realised and the rights that now go with that. As Wayne's wife, I have certain rights that no one else has. I also have the right to carry his name, which I carry very proudly even though only a few can pronounce it properly! I remember practising my new signature for months leading up to our wedding, but it wasn't until the day of our marriage that I was actually entitled to use that new signature and carry that new name!

But I also have the right to a partnership with him in our future together. There are certain things that we will achieve together that we couldn't have achieved individually, and that's exciting! There is a sense of freedom and destiny - a sense that we have a future together that goes beyond just existing - it's the stuff eternity is made of. We're living for a purpose so much greater than ourselves, and we have the kiss of God on our lives! I often have a sense that we are on the greatest adventure together, but with God ultimately, and He's there cheering us on and watching our progress as we forge this life of worship together. In the natural, this is all a mere reflection of the perfect relationship He is waiting for with us individually. And there's no competition!

So the question I need to ask is: Are you in love with your 'husband'? Does your heart beat a little quicker when you think of Him, spend time with Him, and sense Him drawing close to you? Or is your identity as the Bride of Christ tied up in something you DO, rather than who you ARE in relationship to Him? Because honestly, that's never going to cut it.

But it starts with a choice… and that choice is always in response to an invitation…

My greatest love…

In the midst of writing this book, I had a dream just as I was waking up one morning. There have only been two or three times in my life where I have had a specific prophetic dream that was so real and poignant, and in which God spoke to me so specifically, and they were always at that just waking up point - that slightly surreal place between sleep and wakefulness. Well, this dream was based in a church prayer meeting, a small gathering of about 80 or so people. There were pews, and everyone was sitting and looking towards the front as they prayed, but the atmosphere was not charged with faith or joy. In the dream I stood up and started to pray out loud, declaring the goodness of God, and speaking out His attributes, and I felt the atmosphere start to shift. I kept declaring *"You are…"* statements, but then the declarations became more personal as I prayed out, *"You are my highest joy, You are my greatest love… You are my greatest love…"* Someone started to cry gently as you could feel His presence, and I felt that sense of love and warmth welling up in my heart, as I always do when I take just a second to think of Him and what He means to me. And then in the dream, I heard God gently say to me:

"How? How am I your greatest love?"

It wasn't a rebuke or a challenge, because in the atmosphere of prayer and worship I always feel that so strongly, and it's completely genuine. But it was as if God was saying, *"How are you going to show me?"* Because in the end, a professed adoration and love for God is simply lip service, if not outworked in the physical life, and in our choices, actions and attitudes.

The night before I had been watching an episode of my favourite TV series at the time, and it's a great series - fantastic drama and story line - but has pretty coarse language and some slightly questionable themes. I draw the line at blatantly immoral content in movies and on TV, but I have to be honest, coarse language hasn't really bothered me that much in the past. It was almost as if I felt like my level of spiritual maturity was a shield to anything being let into my spirit - surely my intimacy with Jesus isn't being affected by my choice to watch a great TV drama? Surely one thing has nothing to do with the other… it's amazing how we will justify, though, when it comes to emotional entertainment.

But in this dream, He was saying:

"Would Me being your greatest love stop you watching certain movies or programmes on TV?"
"Would Me being your greatest love stop you making decisions about certain things you are doing, or keep you steadfast to the decisions you have already made?"
"When the challenge comes to give something up, or discipline some area of your life, will you do it, out of love for me, simply because you want to delight and please my heart? Or will you balk at that point and justify that one thing has nothing to do with the other?"

And then I felt Him say:

"Because the greatest joy, delight and intimacy you have ever known, lies on the other side of that decision!"

It was as if God was extending an invitation to me to go deeper with Him. He knew my heart was His, He knew my life has always been sold out for His cause, but He was offering me a chance to find a way to show Him how He was my greatest love - something tangible. He was saying:

"This is the next level in our relationship. SHOW me how I'm your greatest love."

I woke up from that dream, and immediately wrote it all down in my journal while it was fresh, and then asked God to give me some confirmation from the Bible, as I went to have my quiet-time. And I felt Him say:

"Why do you need confirmation of this? This is a great way to live, so why ask for a word to test its truth? You know it's Me!"

And then I went to read my Oswald Chambers excerpt for the day, and I felt God say, *"This is going to speak into this!"* and what was written on the same date, blew my mind...

"We must bring our commonplace life, up to the standard revealed in the High Hour. Never allow a feeling which was stirred in you in the High Hour, to evaporate... Act immediately, do something, if only because you would rather NOT do it. If in a **PRAYER MEETING** God has shown you something to do, don't say - "I'll do it!"; DO IT!... Burn your bridges behind you and stand committed to God by your own act. Never revise your decisions, but see that you make your decisions in the light of the High Hour."[4]

The High Hour speaks to me of the place of revelation, the moment with God when you hear Him speak specifically. Even the fact that my reading for the day mentioned a prayer meeting blew me away. Of course, I immediately decided I would no longer watch my favourite TV series, and rather than feeling disappointed that I didn't get to the end of season one, I felt excited and a sense of anticipation as this was a way I could tangibly show my God how much I loved Him.

I joyfully cried my way through our church staff prayer meeting that morning, I was feeling so emotionally soft in His presence, and could feel His nearness tangibly. And then, that night as I drove to the supermarket, I felt Him say:

"Coffee?"

He wasn't asking me if I'd like a cup, He was asking if I'd like to give it up! The conflict definitely came at that point. There was a very definite push back in my mind, and a moment of teetering on the edge, before I realised again this was a tangible way for me to show Him how much I loved Him, and after that the decision was easy. And as I drove to Creative Ministries the next evening with a pounding, caffeine-withdrawal induced headache, all I found myself saying to Him was, *"I love You, I love You! This headache proves it!"* This may seem ridiculous to some reading this, but for me coffee is huge. It's always been the thing I've justified giving up because I really enjoy it - it really is like a good friend! So I went without coffee for nearly two months simply as a tangible way of showing my Jesus that He was the most important to me. The issue actually wasn't the coffee, because in the grand scheme of things, that's pretty pathetic, but it was the willingness to lay it down for a greater level of intimacy with Him. It was a heart test - and it usually is the seemingly small things that are often the hardest to lay down.

All you need and want...

Towards the end of 2011, I was flying to the Kingdom of Tonga for a Women's Conference with Equippers Church there. On the flight across the Pacific, I was asking the Lord what I was to concentrate on for these women, and I felt this slightly cryptic phrase rolling around in my head:

"People won't know that God is all they need and want, until they DECIDE that God is all they need and want."

I had my Bible open and read Psalms 28:6-7 which said:

"Blessed be God - He heard me praying. He proved He's on my side; I've thrown in my lot with Him. Now I'm jumping for joy, and shouting and singing my thanks to Him." (MSG)

As I mulled that over, I got this very real sense that it's not until we throw our lot in with Him, that we truly begin to see the fruitlessness of living any other way than completely abandoned to Him. It's not until we decide that there's no plan B, no going back, no other option, 'He's it baby', that we realise we don't want to live any other way than completely abandoned to Him! The 'jumping-for-joy, shouting-and-singing-my-thanks-to-Him' response comes AFTER we've thrown in our lot with Him. We won't know that God is all we need and want, until we DECIDE that God is all we need and want!

A couple of weeks later, Wayne and I were in Gisborne working with our Equippers Church team there, and again I was reminded of this whole concept, and felt God speaking to me about the importance of the ONE THING. We all walk our journey of faith and trust in God, but I believe every one of us has to face a ONE THING moment. A moment where the true condition of our hearts is revealed, and we come face-to-face with that thing that is keeping us from knowing that God HIMSELF is truly all we want and need.

One thing…

I love the story of two earthly kings, the first one being acceptable to the people. He looked good, and he carried authority, but he was proud, arrogant, fearful and insecure. He loved man's praise more than God's, and in the end was disqualified by his choices and actions. But the second king was chosen by God. He didn't necessarily have the stature of a king, but he was killing lions and bears and giants by the age of 14. He was anointed as king by Samuel the prophet, and then walked a journey that took him as far away as possible from that calling and destiny in the natural, but straight into the heart and purposes of God. And we know he messed up on that journey, yet he was known as a man after God's own heart.

He was the one who wrote, in Psalms 27:4:

"I'm asking God for <u>one thing, only one thing</u>: To live with Him in His house my whole life long. I'll contemplate His beauty; I'll study at His feet." (MSG)

David found it…
Saul missed it…

Then there was the story of two sisters and a brother. They lived in a poor town, but they had a friend of influence who would come and visit their home on a regular basis. Not only was this man a man of influence, but He was a dear, dear friend and He would stay with them to be refreshed, find solace and companionship. Theirs was a privileged relationship with this man. One day, word was received that He was coming to visit, and preparations were underway. One sister was madly cooking in the kitchen, making sure there was enough food for Him and His entourage, and cleaning the house, while the other was relaxed, calm and unhurried. When He finally arrived, the first sister was distracted and busy in the kitchen, while the other dropped what she was doing and just sat with their guest. Annoyed by her younger sister's laziness and lack of concern, she interrupted them saying, *"Master, don't you care that my sister has abandoned the kitchen to me? Tell her to lend me a hand."*

But Jesus' response to her is laid out in Luke 10:41- 42:

"The Master said, 'Martha, dear Martha, you're fussing far too much and getting yourself worked up over nothing. <u>One thing</u> only is essential, and Mary has chosen it – and it won't be taken from her.'" (MSG)

Mary found it…
Martha couldn't see it…

Saul of Tarsus walked an incredible road. A devout Jew, his life's mandate was to persecute the Christians who claimed Jesus Christ was the Messiah. He was zealous to a fault, a brutal murderer on a religious mission… until he encountered Jesus on the road to Damascus, and his life was turned upside down. A true encounter with Jesus changes everything, if we decide to throw in our lot with Him. Upon the revelation of Jesus as Messiah, the scales of deceit were removed from his eyes, he was filled with the Holy Spirit, and his life turned around. Now his mission had changed. His zeal was for leading people to Christ and preaching The Truth. This was a 180 degree transformation, and the religious leaders he had once followed were not happy. He was beaten, imprisoned, stoned, brutalised, shipwrecked, lied about, and faced death countless times.

Yet, he was the one who wrote in Philippians 3:13-14:

"No, dear brothers and sisters, I have not achieved it, but I focus on this <u>one thing</u>: Forgetting the past and looking forward to what lies ahead, I press on to reach the end of the race and receive the heavenly prize for which God, through Christ Jesus, is calling us." (NLT)

We can read that passage and think that Paul's heart was all about the business of just serving Jesus, getting the job done, and pressing on to reach the finish-line prize, but the precursor to this ONE THING is the passage before it in Philippians 3:7-9:

"I once thought these things were valuable, but now I consider them worthless because of what Christ has done. Yes, everything else is worthless when compared with the infinite value of knowing Christ Jesus my Lord. For His sake I have discarded everything else, counting it all as garbage, so that I could gain Christ and become one with Him... " (NLT)

Paul found it…

Then there was a rich young man, who was a devout follower of religious law. He lived a good life, a moral and upright life. He strove to keep all the commandments of the law laid out before him. He looked good on the outside and had the appearance of an upright citizen. And one day he had the enormous privilege of encountering Jesus walking along the street. This rich young man knew Jesus was a man of religious importance, and he greeted him with great reverence and respect. But obviously a question was burning in his mind - for all his good living and striving, he knew there was a question of monumental eternal importance that needed to be settled in his mind. And seeing Jesus face-to-face, he asked Him, *"Good Teacher, what must I do to get eternal life?"* Jesus, even though knowing this man through and through, still outlined the commandments to him, to which the man replied that he had obeyed every one of them since he was a young boy. And Jesus' response to him, was one of love and an invitation to freedom...

"Jesus looked at him hard in the eye – and loved him! He said, 'There's <u>one thing</u> left. Go sell whatever you own and give it to the poor. All your wealth will then be heavenly wealth. And come, follow me.' The man's face clouded over. This was the last thing he expected to hear, and he walked off with a heavy heart. He was holding on tight to <u>a lot of things</u>, and not about to let go." (Mark 10:21-22 MSG)

The rich young man couldn't attain it...

Jesus met a Samaritan woman at a well, at an unusual time of day. The reason the woman was at the well at an unusual time, was because the usual time, caused her too much pain. She was despised by the Jews, ridiculed, looked down upon and probably talked about by all the other women in her community. That would make for a reasonably tortured life! So she went to draw her water at an unusual time when she knew she would meet no-one, and therefore, would not need to face their ridicule and her pain. But this unusual time, she encountered Jesus! He already knew her, and He knew she was going to be there, though she didn't know that. And as she drew physical water for Him, He drew on her spiritual thirst and offered her living water that would never run out. She was desperate for this never-ending water, especially as she perceived it to mean that she would never have to visit this well again and feel the continual pain and rejection of her fellow Samaritans. But Jesus knew there was something in her that was thirsty for God, for righteousness and truth, but there was also something about her life that was keeping her from that ONE THING. So Jesus went there! He asked her to go and get her husband and bring him to the well. The woman tried to cover up her situation by saying she didn't have a husband, and Jesus countered by saying, *"You're right! You don't have a husband - for you have had five husbands, and you aren't even married to the man you're living with now. You certainly spoke the truth!" (John 4:17-18 NLT)* Jesus, in His kindness and mercy, will always touch on the ONE THING that's keeping us from the ONE THING that really matters.

Many things don't cut it...

Like Martha, we may be busy doing MANY THINGS that keep us from finding the ONE THING that is most important...

Like the rich young ruler, we may have done MANY THINGS RIGHT but there's ONE THING that's keeping us from the ONE THING that's most important...

Jesus is our ultimate example. He said He only did what He saw the Father doing. He was so completely linked to His Father's heart that He saw what His Father saw, He felt what His Father felt, He moved where His Father was moving. Jesus was all God, but living on earth within the confines of humanity. Everything we are subjected to, He needed to be subjected to and overcome as man, without drawing on His rights and power as God. Otherwise He would not have been able to relate to us, or be the victory for broken humanity. And He would take Himself away for times of contemplation, solitude and communion with His Father because this was His lifeline. His relationship with His Father was the most important and precious thing to Him. If it's good enough for Jesus, it has to be the way we live our lives!

Jesus' ONE THING...

This unbroken communion with His Father makes the Garden of Gethsemane make so much more sense. The night before Jesus was to be tried, and condemned to death on the Cross, the Bible says that He was on His knees in the Garden, sweating drops of blood, so great was the anguish of His soul at what He was about to endure. It is a medically documented fact, (a condition called 'hematidrosis') that when someone is under incredible emotional pressure, such as facing one's own death, it is possible for the tiny blood vessels around the sweat glands to constrict and eventually rupture, forcing blood into the sweat glands. Now I always used to wonder why Jesus was under this huge amount of emotional pressure. Of course, He knew what He was about to face the next day, and He knew He wouldn't draw on His supernatural empowering strength as God. And, yes, crucifixion was a horrific and degrading way to die, but some of His own disciples would walk that same journey, Peter was even crucified upside down. So it had to be something more than just the physical death He was facing.

Jesus was on His knees, sweating drops of blood, and asking His Father if it was at all possible, could this cup be taken from Him? In other words, if there was any other way for the sins of the world to be dealt with, could they be? But because of His communion with His Father, and the fact that He only did what He saw the Father doing, and felt His heart, He voiced the unbelievably mind blowing statement/declaration, *"Not my will, but Yours."*

Jesus didn't fear the physical death. He didn't fear the scorn, ridicule, and lashings leading up to His crucifixion. He knew what He was facing, and He knew what the outcome was going to be. He saw the whole picture. The Bible even says that it was for the joy set before Him, that He endured the cross.

So what was causing such huge anguish of soul? Here's my belief - Jesus knew that when He would hang on the Cross the next day, and all the sin of the world would be piled on Him - in essence He would literally become sin - His Father, who He was completely emotionally connected to, would HAVE to turn His back on Him. Holy God could not look upon sin even when the vessel carrying it was His beloved son. That was Jesus' ONE THING. Complete, unbroken, emotional one-ness with His Father. And as He hung on the Cross and cried out, *"My God, my God! Why have You forsaken me?"* He felt every black, dark, evil thing that separation from God causes, took it upon Himself, and His life-line with His Father was broken...

If emotional intimacy with His Father was the ONE THING that sustained Jesus, and then the ONE THING that was taken from Him on the Cross, for our redemption, it must be pretty important and powerful. If that is the ultimate key, afforded for us through the blood of Jesus on the Cross, why would we choose to live any other way than seeking that emotional intimacy with our Father?

Sacrifice is a journey of intimacy...

I don't want to be involved in things that will hurt the heart of my Jesus. Therefore, the boundaries I put in place and decisions I make will guard that relationship with His heart. The personal challenge to give certain things up isn't based in legalism, it is based in a revelation that in order to have greater intimacy with Him, something has to be dethroned in my heart. It is not a chore, but a joy for me to put a boundary around any area of my life that could endanger the freedom of my soul, make Him sad, or potentially hinder greater intimacy with Him. His presence is everywhere, but are we willing to make ourselves more aware of it? When we choose to do so, He responds by showing us the things that could get in the way of that greater level of intimacy with Him. But the choice to respond to that invitation or not, is always ours. If there is anything that is potentially holding your heart, attention or focus, or anything that you're getting some measure of emotional release from, rather than your relationship with Him, can I encourage you to challenge yourself on it? Not out of a sense of legalism and obedience to the rules, but in response to relationship with Him. The greatest intimacy and delight you've ever known with Him just may lie on the other side of that decision...

Chapter 12
Agents of Change

"What a moment, You have brought me to
Such a freedom, I have found in You
You're the Healer, who makes all things new
You have risen, with all power in Your hands
You have given me, a second chance
Hallelujah, hallelujah
> I'm not going back, I'm moving ahead
> I'm here to declare to you, my past is over
> In You, all things are made new
> Surrendered my life to Christ
> I'm moving, moving forward

You make all things new, yes You make all things new
And I will follow You, forward."

- 'Moving Forward' [1]

In my experience, God always makes a way when it seems there isn't one. And God always prepares our hearts for a shift, even if we don't completely realise it until after the fact!

At the beginning of 2010, I sat down on the morning of January 1st, to have my year-defining quiet time with God. It is generally my habit to have this quiet time on New Year's Day, (or thereabouts!) and ask God to show me something prophetically that will define the year. I'm always a little bit excited at the prospect of what He will say. The year before He had shown me a verse in Psalms 2 (MSG) that said, *"What do you want? Name it!"* and there was a very real sense that year that He was allowing me, as His child, to ask anything of my Father, name it specifically, and He would go to work on my behalf!

So you can imagine there was a fair bit of expectation and anticipation, as I sat down with my Bible, and asked God to speak to me prophetically through what I read. It also doesn't take much imagination to sense my disappointment when what He showed me that day was:

"I pray to God - my life a prayer - and **wait for what He'll say and do**. My life's on the line before God, my Lord, waiting and watching till morning." (Psalm 130:5-6 MSG)

To me it seemed slightly unremarkable for a year-defining verse, yet something about the phrase, "...**wait for what He'll say and do**", caught me prophetically at the same time. I continued on, knowing God was speaking, but hoping for something a little more dramatic and exciting, until I read in Psalm 131:3:

"Wait, Israel for God. Wait with hope. Hope now; hope always!" (MSG)

It was clear that this WAS, in actual fact, God's year-defining word for me for 2010. WAIT! I had been hoping for something exciting like 'advance and take territory', or even a repeat of 2009 would have been nice, but, no, it was WAIT! I was almost a little embarrassed when talking with others about what God was saying to each of us, especially when they seemed to be getting these incredible words of victory, faith, and triumph. The conversation would go something like this:

"So, what is God saying to you for this year?"
"Ummmm... wait..." I would mumble, barely audibly under my breath.
"Pardon? I didn't quite catch that?" would be the reply.
"Wait..." would be my slightly louder response.
"Oh sure.....I'll give you a little time to gather your thoughts."
"No, WAIT!" I would exclaim.
"Well, there's no need to be rude about it... I wasn't really THAT interested anyway!"

Conversation over…

Sometimes the word doesn't make sense…

There's always room for a little mirth, but the reality was, I knew God was speaking this to me, and as I allowed myself to delve deeper into this 'weight-y' word, (see what I did there?) God began to unpack it for me. This was not a passive, 'sit-around-on-your-backside-and-do-nothing-all-year' word. God was giving me foresight into what my year could look like, and the fact that it would be very easy to react and respond in the wrong way, if I didn't frame my thinking and my world with these Scriptures. There was a sense of expectation in the waiting. I saw an image of myself sitting on the edge of my seat in anticipation, or in the starting blocks of a race, like a well-seasoned athlete, (admittedly, that image wasn't QUITE so clear!) and I knew God was saying:

"Don't run ahead of me. It would be very easy to make decisions based on what seems right, or on what you can accomplish in your own strength and ability. But in everything that you encounter this year, you need to wait. Wait and watch for what I will say and do. Wait with hope in your heart."

And so began a year I probably wouldn't want to repeat, but am so thankful I walked through, if that makes sense? The first thing I noticed heading into the year, was a sense of unrest in my spirit - a real dissatisfaction and discontent - and I couldn't put my finger on it specifically. I didn't enjoy this feeling because I couldn't settle or relax in the space I was in. I felt like something was shifting and yet I was really happy with where we were at in ministry, and life in general. We were loving being on the pastoral staff at Equippers Church, we were loving the travel and the privilege it was to minister in many different nations. We were loving our Creative

Ministries Team and our involvement there as well. Friendships were great, family was great - everything was GREAT! But something was unsettling me. The last time I remembered feeling that same unrest and disquiet, was in the 18 months leading up to our exit from the Parachute Band. We were loving the season with the band but all of a sudden, I could sense the shift, and knew that God was preparing us to leave.

And that's the key - God was preparing me to shift, to move. Previously, when in the Parachute Band, it was a physical shift, but this time was different because I knew God wasn't calling us to stop doing what we were doing. It was the same feeling, but different circumstances and then, coupled with these verses about waiting, I knew God was up to something, but I had no idea what.

Preparation for change...

My Mum had a Liquid Amber tree on her front lawn which had become stunted in its growth because of its physical position, and the other larger trees overshadowing it. She decided she was going to replant it into a better space where it would receive the sunlight and nutrients it needed, and have room to grow. So she was going to prepare a new spot, dig up the tree and just transplant it. Fortunately, she spoke to a tree-guy first who hastily told her she couldn't just uproot the tree and replant it in one swift movement. He showed her how to cut a space around the roots and prepare the hole that the tree was going to be repositioned into. And for about 6 weeks, while keeping it where it was positioned, they would systematically cut around the roots of the tree, gently severing them, and loosening, fertilising and watering the tree, until the roots were prepared for transplant. The tree was then popped into its new 'home', which had also been fertilised and prepared in advance, and it began to flourish and thrive again.

God is so gracious, He never just uproots and repositions us - He prepares the soil of our hearts first, and loosens the heart-roots that may have become bound, and therefore no longer thriving.

Then the transfer is easy because the preparation has been done well! In this case, I knew it was God preparing ME for something, because Wayne didn't seem to be feeling any of the same stuff I was! And though that unsettling feeling felt the same as when we left the Parachute Band, I knew He wasn't asking me to make an external, positional shift. I realised He was wanting to do something IN me at a deep heart level. It would have been easy to misinterpret the unrest and disquiet as something physical, and rush ahead trying to DO a whole lot of things to quell the unsettling feeling, and miss it altogether.

What I needed to do, and what He was asking me to do, was WAIT…

Discontent is the agent of change…

Discontent and dissatisfaction are the tools God often uses to prepare us, and that preparation never feels particularly easy, because it heralds change and few of us deal very well with change. We like to stay comfortable, with all our 'ducks in a row', and everything figured out in our heads. But God will use external irritants to challenge us and cause us to move, especially in a physical shift. And He will use dissatisfaction and unrest within ourselves, to bring change internally if we allow Him to.

It is a well-known principle that people won't change, until the cost of staying the same is greater than the cost of changing. In other words, there can be so much pressure in many different areas - either physically, mentally or spiritually - that we reach breaking point, and we realise that we need to do something about it, because living with the pressure is not going to be an option for much longer.

Choose change...

Wayne loves his Christmas or New Year 'hangi' with his family. For those of you who are not aware, 'hangi' is a traditional Maori way of steaming food under the ground, in a covered pit. The result is an incredibly tender and smokey-flavoured meal, with a hint of earth in it! On many occasions I have watched as Wayne and his brothers pile their plates with hangi, followed by delicious desserts - trifle, pavlova, strawberries and cream puffs, (NOT cooked in the hangi pit in case you were worried!) and an hour later are literally comatose on couches all around the living room, as their bodies shut down and struggle to cope with the huge intake of food! Every year there is a decision made to eat smaller portions, accompanied by groans of pain, but it hasn't really happened yet. The delight of the food still outweighs the cost of the stomach pain after the fact, hence no change occurs!

I remember as a teenager, getting sunburned many times during a summer season... ON PURPOSE! I would lay out my silver foil mat, (to aid tanning at all angles) slather on the baby oil, and lie out in that sun, just daring it to tan me! If I got to end of the day, with bright red eyelids, and was sore all over, I would feel great, because I knew the result was a great tan. The desire and anticipation of a tan still outweighed the cost of the pain in the buuuuurn, hence no change occurred.

Now, on the other hand, my Dad smoked two packets of cigarettes a day for 55 years - from the age of 14 until he was 71 years old. And one day, after he had tripped over while gardening, and hurt his ribs, the doctor gave him a body scan and discovered a tumour in his lung. Dad gave up smoking just like that! The pleasure he gained from smoking was now over-shadowed by the cost of living with cancer... and I am so thankful, because he lived to see another nine years!

Embrace change, embrace life!

When the pressure is on we have a choice to make - will I live with this discomfort, accept it and just keep on keeping on, or will I embrace change? Well, God had spoken to me about watching and waiting for Him, and I was feeling this unrest within me growing steadily. At first I thought it was because I was just tired after a busy year of ministry. We had been travelling away quite a lot, and I was still homeschooling Gracie and Josh, so I felt like I needed to be the 'earth-mother' at home more that year. In response, I subtly started pulling back from ministry commitments, letting Wayne carry more of that responsibility, so I could be home more, and really dig into our family life and schooling the kids. I felt that I was justified in doing this - surely this was something God was asking me to do; taking care of home and hearth first. Now, I'm not saying this is a wrong decision for some, but for me it has never been something God has specifically called me to do - I have always been graced for full-time ministry and as I have served Him first, (of course using wisdom in the way we conducted our family life), He has taken care of everything else. We've always had the mindset that we're in ministry together as a family anyway, and our kids have flourished in that environment. So why, all of a sudden, was I feeling the need to pull back and let Wayne carry the load? I have to admit, I had had a few people whispering well-intentioned concern about me being too busy etc, and, at first, making this decision seemed to relieve the unrest and heart discomfort I was feeling…

… for about a DAY!

It became clear to me, very quickly, that this was NOT the cause of the unrest, and this became glaringly obvious to me leading up to our Shout conference in the April. The week before, I had found some old emails from people who had been touched by the ministry of the Parachute Band in previous years, and had graciously written to tell us. I was very humbled by their words of encouragement and testimony, and it started me thinking about all that God had led us through in ministry, up to that point - the privilege of touching lives - and all He had put in my hand still to do. As I allowed my mind to reflect, I felt God clearly say to me: *"I've given you a platform. What are you doing with it?"* And yes, it WAS a telling off. I had been sidetracked in my heart. We went into Shout Conference and had the privilege of having Pastor John Bevere as our guest speaker. His first message on opening night cut me to the core, as he talked about serving, and the parable of the talents. He finished off by saying that the man who buried his one talent was like the man who only looked out for himself and his family. It was a like a holy slap to my face… I knew God was talking to me very specifically, and I made a decision in my heart that this would be a year of unquestioned YES.

God had me where He needed me to be, my heart had responded to His urging, and I knew I needed to wait on Him and what He was doing. The sense of unrest I felt didn't go away, but I knew it was part of a bigger picture, and God was wanting to take me deeper.

Unravelled surrender…

There are times in our lives when we walk through different situations, and we are able to maintain a measure of control over the circumstances, and over what we will allow God to do. It's almost as if we stay in a place of protection over our hearts out of fear, or lack of trust in God's character and His ability to hold us safe. But God wants us to become UNRAVELLED. To willingly and in full trust, abandon ourselves to His process. It can be a scary place to be in, but it's actually the safest place to be.

Psalms 46:1-3 says:

"**God is a safe place to hide, ready to help when we need Him. We stand fearless at the cliff-edge of doom, courageous in sea-storm and earthquake, before the rush and roar of oceans, the tremors that shift mountains.**" (MSG)

I believe there are varying degrees of pressure to which we are exposed. I have felt incredible pressure at different times in my life – but times where I have still remained in some semblance of control. Times where I have still sensed the undergirding hand of God holding and guiding me, so I have managed to keep a slight handle on what's going on, and what the result might be. Times where God has spoken words like: *"My grace is sufficient for you"*, or *"You can do all things through Christ who gives you strength"*, or even *"Enlarge your borders, stretch out your tent pegs... grow your capacity!"* There have been times when I've felt His gentle rebuke – *"It's time to grow up"* or, *"Do you REALLY trust me?"*

Get bigger!

All of these 'words of encouragement' from God imply stretch and some effort needed on our part, to let God be God of the journey. In 2007, our Pastor, Sam Monk, had prophetically sensed the need to shift something in the life of Equippers Church, and so had hired the Auckland Town Hall for four Sundays in a row in September. For our team this would mean packing in and out our entire sound and lighting rig each week, when we were used to the comfort of having our own venue and, therefore, the privilege of a bit of a sleep-in! We were also bringing in international guest speakers to preach, and were going to do a special item each Sunday, too, so as a team we were feeling a bit of pressure.

The week leading up to the first Sunday in the Town Hall, Wayne and I were in Brisbane, working with a church music team. We also had Gracie and Josh with us, so I was trying to keep on top of their schooling at the same time. We were due to fly back into Auckland late on the Saturday night, ready for the first early morning pack in, and I remember texting my vocalists from Australia, wanting to ensure everything was ready as I hadn't been there for final rehearsals, and so was generally feeling the pressure. Here I was, in a church in Brisbane, working with their team, yet frantically trying to connect with my own team back home in preparation for this monumental Sunday. At the same time, I was keeping my kids on track with their school, and yes, my friends, I'm ashamed to admit it, but I caved! I 'spat the dummy' and the words left my mouth: *"I DON'T THINK I CAN DO THIS!"* This was a time when, *"My grace is sufficient for you"*, or *"You can do ALL things through Christ..."* would have been greatly appreciated, but do you know what I heard God say?

"GET BIGGER!"

Wow... okay... petulant teenager just got told off! I almost wanted to cry! But embracing what He had called us to do was the ONLY option, so I did. We all did, as a Creative Ministries team, and as a church. And, funnily enough, Pastor Sam's prophetic insight for those four Sundays, framed the future for our church as three years later in 2010, we officially became a 'Church on the move', running all our services in the Auckland Town Hall or alternative venues every week. Those four Sundays in 2007, which seemed so monumentally challenging at the time, caused us to indeed get bigger - in our thinking, in our physical capacity, and in seeing much greater possibilities!

Chaos calls to chaos...

"Consider it a sheer gift, friends, when tests and challenges come at you from all sides. You know that under pressure, your faith-life is forced into the open and shows its' true colours. So don't try to get out of anything prematurely. Let it do its' work so you become mature and well-developed, not deficient in any way." (James 1:2-4 MSG)

In times of pressure, we fully recognise, appreciate, and heroically cling to the truth of this passage. Faith is nearly always forged in the 'pressure-kiln'! When we commit to the journey, and allow God to shape and mould us in adversity, the result is strength in faith, and a determination to keep pushing through. Yes, James 1:2-4 is one of those encouraging scriptures we memorise and quote in the midst of pressure and trial.

But then there's THIS verse:

"Chaos calls to chaos, to the tune of whitewater rapids. Your breaking surf, Your thundering breakers crash, and crush me." (Psalm 42:7-8 MSG)

Breaking surf? Thundering breakers? Crashing, and crushing me? CHAOS CALLS TO CHAOS? This is a totally different picture altogether – this isn't the sweet, almost noble, 'count it all joy' scenario. This is pressure to the absolute max! This is out of control, 'trying-to-do-all-I-can-to-just-keep-my-head-above-water' kind of pressure. This is where we can do nothing BUT abandon ourselves completely, to the hand of Almighty God, and hope we come up for air at the end! And through all this, God is subtle and sometimes a little underhanded in His dealings with us. We think we're signing up for a joy-ride, and it turns out to be a journey we were not expecting or anticipating. Yet God knew all along it's exactly what we needed. We may feel Him calling us to a deeper level of intimacy with Him, and thrill at the thought of delicious times in His presence, but have no anticipation of the journey and process it's going to take to get us to that place. Be careful what you pray for - an honest prayer like, *"Jesus, I just want to reflect You!"* will generally mean an open invitation for God to put you in the fire, and start burning the dross off so you can reflect Him more clearly, as I've already shared in chapter 3.

But back to the story unfolding in 2010...

Enter chaos...

In the midst of unrest, but in my determination to say 'yes' to whatever God had for me, I threw myself full-throttle, into life, church life and itinerant ministry. And that's when chaos started calling to chaos, in the form of seemingly natural events, but events that were all out of my control. And I felt the crash and crush of those thundering breakers in a very real way. If I had been given just a little glimpse of what the next three months would hold, I wouldn't have believed it. But God very rarely does give us that glimpse, and, true to His nature, He just launched me into the deep while His unseen and unfelt hand held me through the chaos.

In those 12 weeks following Shout Conference, and my conscious "*Yes!*" to God, my world was sent into a spin, and I couldn't control any of it. In the midst of the demands of ministry, travel and family, my beautiful Dad became sick and then passed away within three weeks. I spent the greater part of those three weeks after emergency surgery, with my family, at his bedside in hospital, in and then out of the Intensive Care Unit, and finally into palliative care, where we could do nothing but hold his hand, tell him we loved him, and watch him slowly slip away. In the face of debilitating grief, yet wanting to feel normal again, I threw myself full speed back into ministry, leading worship at church the day after Dad's funeral, which also happened to be our very first 'Church on the Move' Sunday in the Auckland Town Hall, with Pastor Reggie Dabbs as our guest speaker.

Three weeks later I realised I wasn't in such a great space emotionally, and needed to take a break to refresh and replenish my grieving heart. At the same time, we were experiencing a hugely crushing financial struggle with loss of income that was out of our control - it was as if God was purposely closing doors, and we couldn't do anything about it. It was the first time I had ever seen Wayne under that amount of emotional, breaking-point pressure, and because of my grieving state, he felt he couldn't burden me, so he was trying to carry it heavily himself. And it was taking its toll on him.

In the midst of all this, that same week, we had our final dress-rehearsal before our annual Women's conference, EquipHer, was due to start in two days' time. A number of our Creative Ministries team members were battling with a real sense of intimidation, and as I was starting to get an inkling of what was going on in the spiritual realm, I felt a new indignation rising in me as we battled over our team in prayer, and broke off the enemy in the Spirit. We had begun to see that God was doing something through these pressures, and had a decision to make - fight, or break! We were determined to stand in faith, and in Jesus as our Rock, regardless of what was going on. That night, as we drove home late from rehearsal but feeling strengthened and a sense of breakthrough, Gracie and I were in a car accident involving four vehicles, in which our car was written off. How obvious was the enemy? And then, just to top it all off, a few weeks later, I found a lump in my breast, and the week between discovery, and the diagnosis and treatment of what was thankfully simply a cyst, was an emotional roller-coaster to say the least as I swung between absolute faith, and fear, with my perceived possibility that I may never see my children walk down the aisle…

Natural and spiritual…

You can look at a journey like this and think, *"Well, that's just life. These are just natural circumstances that everyone walks through"*, and, yes, you would be right. But when there's a sense of unrest and disquiet in your heart before these events occur, and God has spoken a word like 'WAIT' to you, you can be pretty sure that the natural circumstances are being worked into developing something deeper in your heart.

The response to this pressure was to throw myself into the arms of Almighty God, and just hold on for the duration. When thundering breakers are crashing over you, what else can you do? There were honestly times within that journey when I wondered if I was going to completely lose it emotionally. I felt so out of control and detached from myself and my emotions, if that makes any sense? But what the enemy had intended for harm, God could turn around for good, and I determined that that was going to become my confession. I wasn't going to let the enemy rob me, and I wasn't going to allow my emotions to keep me trapped in a cycle of grief, despair and irrational fear. I would walk free, no matter how out of control this felt. And the shift happened that quickly...

Shift happens!

In October of that year, we had the privilege of attending Presence Conference, at Bishop Joseph Garlington's church in Pittsburgh. And that conference was an extremely important week in the chaos of my year. It was as if the year of *'waiting for what God would say and do'* was answered in those few days. Through the powerful ministry of Bishop Mark Chironna in one particular message, this whole year was summed up for me. He spoke of Alvin Tofler's book, 'The Third Wave'[3], the three waves being the Agricultural Age, and the Industrial Age, which in turn ushered in the Information Age, with the discovery and development of the computer, and, therefore, huge and rapid technological advancement. Each of these waves or phases in the development of the civilisation of man, lasted a progressively shorter time than the age before, so rapid was the development of technology after the introduction of machinery and the urbanisation of mankind. The Agricultural Age, moving along at a snail's pace, lasted 5500 years, the Industrial Age, 250 years, and the Information Age, 50-60 years. What Tofler couldn't foresee however, was what lay beyond the Information Age. But futurists, and theorists, and those who sit in the 'think tanks' of secular society, predicting future trends, all agreed that at the stroke of midnight, January 1, 2010, the Information Age ended, and a new age was ushered in that was predicted would last 10 years. No one was willing to predict what would happen beyond those 10 years, and no one was bold enough to name this Age, except for one man, David Houle, who said it would be known as the Shift Age.

Excitement welled up in me as I listened to this message and realised that it was January 1, 2010, that I had heard God say, *"Wait for what I will say and do"*, and my world was sent into an absolute spiral of uncertainty, undergirded with this uncomfortable feeling of unrest and shift. NOW it all made sense!

Ushering in the new age...

What's more David Houle believed that the Global Financial Crisis between 2007-2009 really heralded this Shift Age. And, looking back, I could see correlation of this shift in my own life personally. It was at the beginning of 2007, after a period of restlessness and discontent, that Wayne and I left the incredible season with the Parachute Band, and joined our voluntary staff at Equippers. It was like a coming-home for us, and life became wonderfully full and busy - I had gone from touring three weeks at a time, and being simply a full-time Mum at home in between tours, to full-time, 24/7 ministry while consumed with kids, schooling, as well as the temporal, everyday things right in front of me. And, in all honesty, as life suddenly started moving at an exponential pace, I had unconsciously been letting the 'urgent rob the important'. In about July of 2007, we had the opportunity to be in Kuala Lumpur, Malaysia, as a family, working with a church there. One morning I woke well before dawn, and, as I couldn't get back to sleep, I got up and opened our curtains. As I looked out of our hotel window at this darkened city caught in the grip of Islam, I felt such a deep prophetic stirring in my spirit, and felt God clearly say to me:

"Set your face like flint to do my will. These are urgent days. Time is your most precious commodity - don't waste it!"

This word was a real wake-up call - how could I be so consumed with the everyday, temporal things of my comfortable New Zealand, Christian existence, worrying about things I had no right to be worrying about? Absorbed with my own 'first-world' problems when the reality for countless millions of people in nations around the world, was an eternity of darkness, and the living hell on earth of gross poverty and oppression? I felt overwhelmed, and I texted my lovely friend Karo, who said, she had literally just been thinking of me at that moment, (time zone difference!) and sensed God really wanted to speak to me clearly in my quiet time that morning. So as I sat on the bathroom floor of our hotel room, with barely a sliver of light shining, I opened my Bible and the first thing I read was Colossians 3:1-3:

"So if you're serious about living this new resurrection life with Christ, ACT like it. Pursue the things over which Christ presides. Don't shuffle along, **eyes to the ground, absorbed with the things right in front of you. Look up, and be alert to what is going on around Christ** - that's where the action is. See things from His perspective." (MSG)

It seems to be that when God does something in the spiritual, there is a mirroring in the natural. While the financial crisis of 2007-2009 ushered in the Age of Shift in the natural, at the beginning of 2010, I believe God was preparing many, many Christians in the spirit at the same time. This preparation seemed to be a challenge to live with uncertainty, to embrace change, and to be ready to move when He spoke…

If you're serious about Christ… ACT LIKE IT!
Stop being absorbed with the temporal things right in front of you…
Look up and be alert…
See things from HIS perspective…

I have spoken to so many people who have felt this same shifting and unsettling feeling around the same time. It's as if the timeline in the Spirit had been mirrored in the natural, not the other way around! I love the fact that our pastor prophetically felt that something needed to shift in the life of our church in 2007, and, in 2010, we became the Church on the Move, without the certainty of an established church home, but holding our services in the Auckland Town Hall weekly. Why move from a building you own and are comfortable and secure in, to the uncertainty of changing venues, and the added pressure of a huge pack-in and out every week? But that move in the natural, was mirroring something that was already happening in the spirit. In the natural it didn't make sense, financially it definitely didn't make sense, yet I believe it was all preparation to be a part of this spiritual Age of Shift, and Pastor Sam was seeing it prophetically. Added to that, many years ago, massive revival broke out in the Auckland Town Hall, and we are now seeing a 're-digging' of those wells in that same venue! God is doing something exciting and fresh, and, in the midst of the uncertainty, He is building and using His Church!

The fact is, as Christians who have the mind of Christ, we need to be people who can live with uncertainty in the natural, and be willing to go where God calls us to go, and do what He calls us to do. The only certain thing is that God is seated on the throne, and He knows EXACTLY what is going on. He is our Rock, His Holy Spirit is our guide, and we can walk with absolute assurance that He is in control and guiding our every step, even when we can't see for the fog in front of us.

These are urgent days we are living in. These are exciting days we are living in. I fully believe that God is preparing a company of Christians for the next coming Apostolic Reformation. We are 500 years from the Reformation of Martin Luther, Calvin and Zwingli, when God shook the Church and the wrong ideologies and man-based theories that had become ingrained as law in church culture. He's shaking the Church again, and these are the days we're living in NOW! I don't know about you, but that excites me beyond measure - what a privilege to be called for such a time as this!

You are part of the most exciting days in the history of the Church... will you be part of that company who can live with uncertainty, embrace change and do the Father's bidding without hesitation?

If so, welcome to the journey of a lifetime…

References

Chapter One - The Journey Begins

1. Huirua, Libby. (2010). Breathe. On *We Won't be Silent*. © 2010 Equippers Church (Admin. by Equippers Church Auckland) (p) 2010 Equippers Church
2. THE MESSAGE. Copyright © 1993, 1994, 1995, 1996, 2000, 2001, 2002. Used by permission of NavPress Publishing Group.

Chapter Two - A Season to Grow

1. *The Holy Bible, New King James Version(r)*. Copyright © 1982 by Thomas Nelson, Inc. Used by permission. All rights reserved.
2. Chambers, Oswald. *My Utmost for His Highest*. © 1935 by Dodd Mead & Co., renewed © 1963 by the Oswald Chambers Publications Assn., Ltd. Used by permission of Discovery House Publishers, Grand Rapids.

Chapter Three - Deeper

1. Huirua, Libby. (1998). Deeper. On *Adore*. © 1998 Parachute Music (Admin. by EMI Christian Music Publishing). (p) 1998 Parachute Records Inc.
2. Indescribable. Loiue Giglio. Chordant / EMI. 2012. DVD.
3. Parachute Band. (1999). *You Alone*. (p) 1997 Parachute Records Inc.
4. Holy Bible, New Living Translation, copyright ©1996, 2004, 2007, 2013 by Tyndale House Foundation. Used by permission of Tyndale House Publishers, Inc., Carol Stream, Illinois 60188. All rights reserved.
5. NET Bible® copyright © 1996-2006 by Biblical Studies Press, L.L.C. All rights reserved.
6. THE HOLY BIBLE, NEW INTERNATIONAL VERSION (R), NIV (R), Copyright © 1973, 1987, 1984 by International Bible Society (R), used by permission. All rights reserved worldwide.

7. The NIV Worship Bible, New International Version © 2000 by The Corinthian Group, Inc. All Rights Reserved. Quote by Arthur T. Pierson

Chapter Four - God Knows What He's Doing!

1. Huirua, Libby. (2014). Grace. On *Journey.* © 2014 Wayne and Libby Huirua

Chapter Five - How Can I Not Sing?

1. Huirua, Libby, Huirua, Wayne. (2008). Worthy. On *Can you feel it.* © 2008 Equippers Church (Admin. by Equippers Church Auckland) (p) 2008 Equippers Church
2. AMPLIFIED BIBLE, Copyright © 1954, 1958, 1962, 1964, 1965, 1987 by The Lockman Foundation. All rights reserved. Used by permission.

Chapter Six - It All Begins in the Mind

1. Huirua, Libby, De Jong, Mark, Huirua, Wayne. (1999). All my life. On *Love.* (2000). © 1999 Integrity's Praise! Music (Admin. by Crossroad Distributors Pty. Ltd.) Parachute Music (Admin. by SHOUT! Music Publishing). (p) 2008 Parachute Records.
2. Dr. Cho, David Yonggi. (1987). *The Forth Dimension: Discovering a New World of Answered Prayer.* By Bridge-Logos.

Chapter Seven - Expensive Worship

1. Pasley, Ben. (2001). *Enter the Worship Circle.* © 2001 by Relevant Media Group, Inc.
2. Bishop Garlington, Joseph. (1997). *Worship: The Pattern of Things in Heaven.* © Copyright 1997 - Destiny Image Publishers.
3. Lewis, C.S. http://cslewis.com/
4. Huirua, Libby. (2007). Saving Arms. On *Revolution.* © 2010 Equippers Church (Admin. by Equippers Church

Auckland) (p) 2007 Equippers Church.

Chapter Eight - Created for One-ness

1. Prothero, Jonathan, Huirua, Wayne. (2012). Overwhelmed. On
2. *Light it up.* © 2012 Equippers Church (Admin. by Equippers Church Auckland) (p) 2013 Equippers Church
3. The Shorter Catechism. © 1970 by G.I. Williamson. One-volume edition © 2003.
4. Webster, Merriam. (2004). *The Merriam-Webster Dictionary.* Springfield, MA: Merriam-Webster Inc.

Chapter Nine - My Soul Sings

1. Huirua, Libby. (2008) Spoken message to Ministry team
2. NOOMA Complete Collection. Rob Bell. Zondervan. 2014. DVD.
3. Huirua, Libby, Huirua, Wayne. (2008). My Soul Sings. On *Can You Feel It* . © 2008 Equippers Church (Admin. by Equippers Church Auckland) (p) 2008 Equippers Church
4. Eldredge, John. (2001). *Wild At Heart.* Nashville: Thomas Nelson.

Chapter Ten - Living Building Stones

1. Lindsey, Aaron, Houghton, Israel, Sims, Tommy. (2010). Love God, Love People. On *Love God, Love People.* (c) © 2010 Ardent Media (Admin. by Crossroad Distributors Pty. Ltd.) Integrity's Praise! Music (Admin. by Crossroad Distributors Pty. Ltd.) Sound Of The New Breed (Admin. by Crossroad Distributors Pty. Ltd. Remaining portion is unaffiliated. (p) 2010 Integrity Media, Inc.
2. Prison Break. (2005, 29th August). TV programme. Fox.

Chapter Eleven - It's All About Jesus

1. Ranney, Adam, Houghton, Israel, Massey, Micah. (2011). Jesus at the Centre. On *Jesus at the Centre.* © 2011 Integrity's Praise! Music (Admin. by Crossroad Distributors Pty. Ltd.)

Sound Of The New Breed (Admin. by Crossroad Distributors Pty. Ltd.) Regenerate Music Co. (Admin. by Watershed Music Co.) Remaining portion is unaffiliated. (p) 2012 RGM New Breed / Integrity Music

2. Equippers Creative Lab is the Creative Arts School based out of Equippers Church, Auckland and founded in 2014 by Wayne and Libby Huirua

3. King, Ross. (2002). Clear the Stage. On *And All the Decorations, Too.* © 2002 Ross King Music (Admin. by Crossroad Distributors Pty. Ltd.) Simple Tense Songs (Admin. by Crossroad Distributors Pty. Ltd.) (p) 2002 Ross King. All rights reserved. Unauthorized reproduction is a violation of applicable laws. Distributed by Catapult.

4. Chambers, Oswald. *My Utmost for His Highest.* © 1935 by Dodd Mead & Co., renewed © 1963 by the Oswald Chambers Publications Assn., Ltd. Used by permission of Discovery House Publishers, Grand Rapids.

Chapter Twelve - Agents of Change

1. Houghton, Israel, Sanchez, Ricardo. (2007). Moving Forward. On *The Power of One.* © 2007 Integrity's Hosanna! Music (Admin. by Crossroad Distributors Pty. Ltd.) Integrity's Praise! Music (Admin. by Crossroad Distributors Pty. Ltd.) New Breed Extended (Admin. by Crossroad Distributors Pty. Ltd.) Ricardo Music Dot Com (Admin. by Crossroad Distributors Pty. Ltd.) Sound Of The New Breed (Admin. by Crossroad Distributors Pty. Ltd.). (p) 2009 Integrity Media, Inc.

Made in the USA
San Bernardino, CA
16 September 2016